Saviors

Saviors

Beyond Qumran, Nag Hammadi, and The New Testament Code

Robert Wahler

Library of Congress Control Number: 2009905850
ISBN: Hardcover   978-1-4415-4569-5
                  Softcover   978-1-4415-4568-8

To order additional copies of this book, contact:

Xlibris Corporation
1-888-795-4274
www.Xlibris.com

Orders@Xlibris.com
57180

Contents

Dedicated to Robert Lopp, Dawn Wilson,
and all the members of the Local Churches.

What I've said is that people mistake literature for history.
Robert H. Eisenman, interviewed by Rachael Kohn on
"Spiritual Things" radio program in Australia 7 August, 2005

For this is the will of my Father, that every one who SEES the Son
and believes in him should have everlasting life;
and I will raise him up on the last day.
John 6:40

For the Guide [the Leader of the Qumran community] *in order to communicate and teach all the Sons of Light the history of THE SONS OF MAN,* [teaches] *according to all the kinds of their spirits, the signs concerning their works and their generations, and the Visitation of their punishments and the Eras of their reward.* Community Rule III:13-14, Dead Sea Scrolls

Introduction

"'And he opened his mouth and taught *them,* saying:'" and, again: "'And he opened *his mouth* and taught them, *saying:*'" Matthew 5:2 (RSV).

Jesus taught *them,* not us, and *by word of mouth,* not by the written word.

If one is willing to suspend unbelief long enough to consider what the historic Jesus Christ actually taught, not what is generally assumed to be what he might have said or written, one will see a remarkable Truth. The Message of God for mankind has been coming to our world not just in the person of Jesus Christ but from many others entirely his equal in both power and grace. I'm not trying to convert anyone to anything. I only wish to show that the Gospel writers and Jesus himself demonstrated, in various instances in the Gospels, that his ministry was a verbal and time-and-place limited one, and indicated clearly that he was not alone in coming here as Savior. I have no original research to contribute, only a few original exegeses of parables such as David and Goliath and verses such as Acts 4:8-12, Daniel 7:27, and Deuteronomy 11:18. What I do offer is a broad overview of

Middle Eastern religious scripture, an understanding of Eastern religion, and how the two seamlessly mesh. I see myself as a sort of "traffic cop" of materials, sorting out insightful from uninspired, putting together sources which when put together show what we need to know. There is a persistent myopia in the West to things Eastern that must be addressed, as the key to fully understanding the message of ancient biblical scripture is to be found there. Having come to this as a devoted one-time Christian myself—but not as a scholar—I am not a Bible expert, but believe I do know it well enough to make a contribution to understanding its message. I lived and breathed the Bible—years ago—and still revere the words of Jesus. I know that believers tend to reject anything challenging the sole supremacy of their Master, but one has to accept with an open mind what it is that *he himself* might have said about his mission here on earth. To do less denies his Godhood.

The reality of who Jesus Christ was, if indeed he existed at all, and what he is reputed to have taught have been persistently misrepresented from the very beginnings of the written gospels. My goal is to bring the import of both long-standing traditions not well known to the public at large and new discoveries that bear upon the understanding of these teachings to front and center in the debate over who and what the real Jesus Christ might have been. This is the true story of Jesus Christ's ministry as well as can be constructed from historical sources. It is also the true story of others—close relatives—who brought that same gospel. Start with no assumptions except that Jesus Christ lived, and had kin. There could be one, none, or many, Saviors. His own words (or those said to be his), and those of others close to him will tell you. A few concepts to help understand—like karma and reincarnation—are also shown in his teachings. If something is interpreted, like "light" in John 1:8-9, it is to clarify how it fits with other verses to illustrate a point. All scripture italics are mine.

> *"In religion and politics, people's beliefs and convictions are in almost every case gotten at second-hand, and without examination, from authorities who have not themselves examined the questions at issue but have taken them at second-hand from other non-examiners, whose opinions about them were not worth a brass farthing".*
> —Mark Twain's Autobiography, 1959

Chapter One

The Saviors

Jesus the Nazoraean

Jesus, Matthew 1:21: "'she will bear a son, and you shall call his name Jesus, for he will save *my people* from their sins.'"

"*My*" people, not "*his*" or "*the*" people. So is introduced the Savior Jesus Christ to the world by (the writer of) The Gospel According to Matthew. Scholars are not certain who wrote Matthew. It is not well known that original Matthew was likely in Hebrew, not Greek (per Origen, Eusebius, and Irenaeus—covered below), though no extant copies are known, and this is only the first of the many alterations to "scripture" to have occurred through its many permutations. The changes are without exception always *toward* a reading of the exclusivity of Jesus as Savior, never away from it to one of manifold incarnations. We will see this over and over throughout the New Testament. Three more Gospels follow. (Matthew includes the "fall of the Temple" prophecy, but not the event—it hadn't occurred yet when it was written, and Matthew is known for his penchant of reporting fulfilled prophecy. It was therefore written prior to 70 CE. The virgin birth fiction in Greek Matthew is absent in the Hebrew, which adds to its authenticity and earlier dating. Hebrew Matthew also explains the absence of The Sermon on the Mount in Greek Mark, usually said to predate *Greek* Matthew.) Mark was not a close associate of Jesus, and may or may not have authored the Gospel. He was—according to historian Eusebius Pamphilius—Peter's companion and interpreter. The Gospel According to Luke may or may not have been written by Luke, also not a close associate of Jesus—he was Paul's traveling companion (and also, it is commonly presumed, wrote The Acts of the Apostles). The Gospel According to John, modern scholars believe, was written anonymously by a non-eyewitness, some 60 years after Jesus' death, and may well be a completely allegorical work not based on witnesses at all, but upon a general (and commanding) understanding of his life and teachings. Of the twenty-seven books in the New Testament, only seven are widely believed to be attributable to their purported authors, all Paul: his letters to the Romans, Corinthians (1 & 2), Galatians, Philippians, 1 Thessalonians, and Philemon. All the others are either definitely not authentic or are debatable. In these times it was common to write pseudonymously. Paul's letters are earliest, and perhaps contemporary with Q ("Quelle," meaning "source") and the Gospel of Thomas. We'll do the best we can with them. The Revised Standard Version (RSV) and the Authorized (King James) Version (KJV) of the Holy Bible will be our primary guides. Newly discovered apocrypha (non-canonical source material), primarily the books of the Dead Sea Scrolls from Qumran on the Dead Sea, and the Nag Hammadi Library from Nag Hammadi, Egypt, will provide support, as will leading experts from the field of biblical textual criticism. The experts chosen are considered "leading" in this author's opinion because they have done the most to reveal the problems inherent in a literal or face-value reading of extant scriptures.

Jesus, Mark 10:45: "'For the Son of Man came not to be served but to serve, and to give his life a ransom *for many.*'" Not "all" but "*many*"—will be ransomed, *and by his life, not his death* (to be explained later). His mission was the salvation of His *given* souls, *not* the souls of everyone to ever be "saved."

Jesus, John 6:40: "'For this is the will of my Father, *that every one who sees the Son* and believes in him should have eternal life; and I will raise him up at the last day.'" He was *talking* to his audience. *He did not write that.* He was giving a description of the Father's will. And saying it in Aramaic (or possibly Hebrew) but not in Greek or English! If elsewhere he says believe and be saved, he doesn't say "see" and believe, because it is understood that someone "sees" who is speaking to them (unless they're *blind*). Don't torture what he said to fit a preconception which is at odds with this, for example: "'We must work the works of him who sent me, *while it is day* ["while I'm alive"]; night ["death"] comes, when no one can work. *As long as I am in the world*, I am the light of the world'" (John 9:4-5). Why does he say that if he continues to be the light after he is gone? It isn't because the Comforter he sends is going to be the light—Jesus and the Holy Spirit are *One*. He is the light of the world for *only* his followers—*not* others'. When he says "last day" he means the day of one's death—not the apocalyptic "end of the world." "Day" in John 9:4 is "lifetime," because, of course, many people have night "work." "Night" is, therefore, death ("when *no one* can work"). Annotated RSV Bibles show the footnote for "me" in John 9:4 as "Other ancient authorities read '*us*'"—"'We must work the works of Him who sent *us* while it is day; night comes, when no one can work'" which is a more logical construction, if for no other reason than that it makes more sense of the limitation Jesus himself puts upon himself ("night comes, when no one [including Jesus] can work"), and is also to be preferred over the Authorized (King James) Version, "'*I* [singular] must work the works of him who sent me, while it is day; the night cometh when no man can work.'"—clearly showing someone was uncomfortable, in *both* versions, with the idea of multiple Christs!

Look at the context. John 6:

[35] "Jesus said to them, 'I am the bread of life; he who comes to me shall not hunger, and he who believes in me shall never thirst.

[36] But I said to you that you have seen me *and yet do not believe.*

[37] All that the Father gives me will come to me; and him who comes to me I will not cast out.

[38] For I have come down from heaven, not to do my own will, but the will of him who sent me;

[39] and this is the will of him who sent me, that I should lose nothing of all that he has given me, but raise it up at the last day.

[40] For this is the will of my Father, *that every one who sees the Son* and believes in him should have eternal life; and I will raise him up at the last day.'"

Jesus tells the crowd they see "and yet do not believe." *He means see with your eyes.* He means *see physically*, not metaphorically, or "in one's heart" or "see Christ in others"—as some would have it, because "you have seen me and yet do not believe" shows his intended audience is only those *listening,* not others who might claim possibly seeing him only within. Then, in the same lesson—without interruption or changing subjects—he says it is "the will of my Father, that every one who sees the Son and believes in him" will be saved. This is positive *proof* that Jesus Christ taught a ministry limited to those who were alive when he was. He is saying that if they don't *see* him, he cannot save them. There is only one way of reading this exchange, and it clearly shows what Jesus was trying to say. He says *one needs to see him* to partake of the salvation he offers. That is what *he says* is "the will of my Father." (The verbs here, "sees" and "believes," are actually mistranslated. They should be rendered from John's original Greek into the English continuous present tense: "is seeing" or "continues to see" and "is believing" or "continues to believe." Young's Literal Translation has "is beholding" and "is believing": "'and this is the will of Him who sent me, that every one who is beholding the Son, and is believing in him, may have life age-during, and I will raise him up in the last day.'" This implies a continuous "seeing" and "believing" with a deeper mystical meaning, and will be taken up in the next chapter.)

Many phrases Jesus used, such as "while it is day," were obviously allegorical. Jesus, Matthew 16:28: "'Truly, I say to you, there are some *standing here* who will not taste death before they see the Son of man coming in his kingdom.'" This verse confirms that "the last day" doesn't mean The Apocalypse, because it didn't happen in the time of Jesus (nor has it yet!). The "*standing* here" word-form is in itself significant, as will be discussed later in this chapter. John 5:25: "'Truly, truly, I say to you, the hour is coming, *and now is* [not waiting for the "end of the world"], when the dead will hear the voice of the Son of God, and those who hear will live [resurrect].'" The terrible things described in Matthew 24 are a description of the developing state of affairs in first century Roman-ruled Palestine. And the Gospel *did* get preached (v 14) through the whole known world of the time. Some reading this think things are getting bad *now?* Read accounts of life in Roman times for non-Romans. It was no picnic. The Jewish revolt and subsequent destruction of Jerusalem and the Temple in 66-70 CE, the result of the death of James—as we will discuss later (not anything to do with Jesus) is what is described in Matthew 24, not a "final apocalypse" for our time. Judaism in Roman Palestine was tolerated by the Romans, but the Jews, looking for a Messiah—and most rejecting Jesus—were to reject his followers, too. Jesus was merely warning them of trials to come. The second half of the chapter, from verse 27 on is a description of internal experiences of a disciple when the Savior comes at "the last day" *of his or her life,* not "the end of the world." This is also the meaning of "the latter days" whenever you read that. *Your* latter days are when you are near death! *Your* last day is the day you die! There is no "final day" universal salvation—there never has been, and never will be—in spite of all the Raphaels and Michelangelos. "The dead" and "the voice of the Son of God" here are not what you may think. They are the *living,* dead *in spirit,* and the Spirit (or *"Word"*) of God, which will be discussed in chapter two.

If anyone missed 16:28, J̶o̶h̶n̶ [Matthew] has Jesus again saying:

"'Truly, I say to you, *this generation* will not pass away till all these things take place'" (Matthew 24:34). "This generation" is, of course, the one *to which he was speaking*. Where is there reference to another? The "lesson of the fig tree" meaning Israel is mere speculation. It refers to the inner experience of seeing Christ come *within* (v 30: "'Then will appear the sign of the Son of man *in heaven* [*within* you—*not* 'in the sky']'") at the time of one's death. He wasn't *writing* that. He was *speaking* to those *listening to him. They weren't going to be here* to see Israel become a nation in 1948. He was teaching *an audience* about salvation and what happens to the individual who is saved. Remember that whenever you read the words of Jesus Christ! He never wrote *anything* to us. Verses 36-44 describe when Jesus' given disciples are *to die* and "see Christ." He was to "come" (in spirit) at a time "they would not expect" (v 44): their *death!*

Jesus did tell his disciples at the Last Supper that He was "the way." "'I am the way, and the truth, and the life, no one comes to the Father, but by me'" (John 14:6). *But then he says*, "'If you had known me, you would have known my Father also; henceforth, you know him *and have seen him*" (John 14:7). Again, he was speaking *to those who were present*—no one else! He was "the way" *for them*, and *only* them. John 15:13: "'Greater love has no man than this, that a man lay down his life *for his friends.*'" And who does Jesus say *they* are?

Next verse: "'*You* are my friends if *you* do what I command you.'" He was *speaking* to his *disciples*—not you! Somebody else (John) was doing the writing. Also, verse 20: "'Remember the word I *said* to you'"; verse 22: "'if I had not come *and spoken* to them'"; verse 24: "'*now they have seen me* and hated both me and my Father.'" Jesus never said to somebody "Go write this down to everyone who will ever live, to read and make their own!" "His own" were there with him—*in person.*

Jesus, John 17:2 (KJV): "'since thou [Father] hast given him [Jesus] power over all flesh, to give eternal life to *all whom thou hast given him*.'" The Gospels called it "*Baptism*"—The Master connecting his chosen disciples with himself through the Holy Spirit.

Verse 4: "'I glorified [past tense] thee on earth, having accomplished [present perfect tense] the work which thou gavest [past tense] me to do.'"

Verse 6: "'I have manifested [present perfect tense] thy name [Holy Spirit] to the men that thou gavest [*past* tense] me out of the world; thine they were [past tense], and thou gavest [past tense] them to me, and they have kept [present perfect tense] thy word [Holy Spirit].'"

Verse 9: "'I am praying for them; I am not praying for the world, but for those whom thou hast given [present perfect tense] me, for they are thine; all mine are thine, and thine are mine, and I am glorified in them.'" Jesus Christ's work was initiating those souls given him by the Father. Not those souls who would or could be given, but just "given"—*past tense.* "Having accomplished the work" is present perfect tense—*the work is done.* Jesus Christ cannot "save" anyone now. He can't even if he wanted to—elsewhere in the Gospels he says he is powerless to do anything other than the will of the Father (John 6:38).

Verse 11: "'And now I am no more in the world, *but they are in the world*, and I am coming to thee.'" "They" are none other than "the given"—right? If they are "in the world" they can't be those yet to be born—right? His "saved" souls were *all* in the world as he *spoke* these wonderful words. He wasn't "praying" for the world, or for me or for you, but for "they" who were *"in the world"*—two thousand years ago.

John the Baptist

It is no accident Jesus uses "we" in John 9:4.

John 1:6-7: "'There was a man sent from God whose name was *John*. He came for testimony, to bear witness to the light that all might believe through *him*.'" No Jesus yet—"him" is John! How could "him" refer to Jesus when Jesus has not even been introduced?

John 1:8: "'He was not that light, but came to bear witness to the light.'" "Light," here, doesn't refer to Jesus or John, but God.

John 1:9: "'That was the true light that lights every man who comes into the world.'" The light is God—because Jesus doesn't light "every man" who comes into the world—God does.

John 1:12: "'But to all who received him, who believed in his name [the 'Word'], he gave *power* to become children of God.'" He took them as *his* disciples. *He* gave the power, *not* Jesus. John 1:6-13 are *all* about John the Baptist. It was John doing the giving. Jesus is not mentioned in this chapter until the 14th verse: "'*And* the Word became flesh and dwelt among us, full of grace and truth; we have beheld his glory, glory as of the only Son [meaning "Spirit"—explained later] from the Father.'" John (the author) is telling his readers that John the "Baptist" (only Christ "baptizes") was a Christ. This is critically important. The conjunctive word "And" denotes a *new* subject (see "Greek Bible Study" website, and "Net Bible" footnote 34 on John 1:14). Some Bibles break the paragraph *after* verse 14. No. If there is a transition from Spirit to Savior in verse 14, verse 10 must be describing a *different* Savior, because the introduction of Jesus in verse 14 by way of verse 15 would have to refer *back to before* verse 14 to verse 11 "'He [until now, the Spirit] came to his own home, and his own people [the Spirit is *now* incarnate] received him not'" for that to be true. This isn't the way to read John. There must be *two* Saviors in this prologue, not just one—John *and* Jesus. Using "And" to lead a sentence is apparently a common sentence construction in antiquity—especially Greek—but not today. Many miss its significance because it *is* so uncommon. It is an ancient *segue*.

John the Baptist, John 1:15: Read carefully: "'This is he of whom I said, "After me comes a man who ranks before me, for *he was* [existed] before me"'" means they both were with the Father before either was born—not that he was less, in some way, than Jesus. John 1:35: "The next day again John was standing with two of *his* disciples." Before Andrew and (probably) his brother Simon Peter (John 1:40) were followers of Jesus they were *disciples* of John. Who else in the Bible has *disciples*, but "Christ" (except for a delusional Paul!—Acts 9:24)? Go to Matthew 3:10 and see where John says, "'*Even now* the ax is laid to the root of the trees; every tree therefore that does not bear good fruit is cut down and thrown into the fire.'" John is telling the Sadducees and Pharisees that the time is *now* to choose salvation, not later, and he is their Savior (not Jesus).

Now for something undeniably revealing. Jesus himself introduces the existence of other Masters:

Jesus, John 3:11: "'*We* speak of what *we* know, and bear witness to what *we* have seen; but you do not receive *our* testimony.'" Who are "*we*"? The only other person he speaks of by name in this chapter is Moses (v 3:14). In verse 19 Jesus says "'And this is the judgment, that the light has come into the world and men loved darkness rather than light, because their deeds were evil'" implying he is speaking of someone *who came before him* ("loved" is past tense)—presumably John the Baptist. You now see *Jesus* speaking of other Saviors! *Moses*—as well as John the Baptist—was also a "Savior" (a "Christ" or a "Master")! We now have three! (More on Moses as Master later.) The Father is the "Word" (John 1:1) and the "Word" (John 1:12 ["name" means "Word"—more on that later] and 1:14) is in turn, the incarnate, human, Masters. One may want to say Jesus is speaking for his disciples as well as himself, but they were as yet new to the teachings themselves, and not likely to know much more than the audience. In any case, they weren't yet "speaking."

It is a curious thing that everyone sees John as "the Baptist" but no one sees him as Savior in his own right. Anyone who truly "baptizes" is a Savior. John the Baptist again, John 3:30: "'He must increase, but I must decrease.'" This is very significant. Apparently John thought himself equal to Jesus, or at the least a possible interference for Jesus as he began his ministry. Even Luke slips a little as he acknowledges John's preeminence with this (11:1-4), "He [Jesus] was praying in a certain place, and when he ceased, one of his disciples said to him, 'Lord, teach us to pray, *as John taught his disciples to pray.*'"Then follows, "'Father, hallowed be thy name. Thy kingdom come'" and the rest of the famous Lord's Prayer—*which was John's* before it was his. "Preparing the way" of Isaiah 40:3: "A voice cries: 'In the wilderness prepare the way of the Lord, make straight in the desert a highway for our God'" has a much deeper significance than "setting the stage for Jesus" as will be seen later regarding the "wilderness camps" in the desert at Qumran, and is not likely prophecy at all, but if it is it is foretelling John himself or even more likely James, Jesus' brother, as both were more associated with "wilderness" ministries than was Jesus, although Jesus sought refuge there too. "The Way" is observing the Torah, or even simply the Master as in John 14:6. "Preparing the way" is setting one's heart on God, and involves only Master and disciple—not herald and Master. The "crying voice" of Isaiah 40:3 is the "Word" (or "name"—"hallowed" in John's prayer above) as shown by Isaiah 40:6: "A voice [not John's] says "Cry!" Malachi 3:1: "Behold, I send my messenger to prepare the way before me, and the Lord whom you seek will suddenly come to his temple; the messenger of the covenant in whom you delight, behold he is coming says the Lord of hosts" is also conflated into "a prophecy" of Christ's coming, when it really is an allusion to what happens within the disciple when he is ready at the time *any* Master comes: "the messenger *in whom you delight* [the 'Word'] *suddenly* comes [within] to *his temple* [the body]." The "messenger" is the Holy Spirit in the person of the *Master*. This is not a herald of a coming Messiah, but a mystic coming of the Lord within as Holy Spirit or "name" as Malachi elsewhere calls Him.

Then—lacking quotation marks—John 3:31-36 shows John the Baptist speaking.

"'He who comes from above *is above all;* he who is of the earth belongs to the earth, and of the earth he speaks; he who comes from heaven is above all. He bears witness to what he has seen and heard, yet no one receives his testimony'" (John 3:31-32). This was *spoken* by John the Baptist. It shows two things, both very important. One, only one who has seen heaven for oneself could in all seriousness write or say that—showing John the Baptist (*or John the Apostle, which is less likely*) must be *a Master himself*. And two, that the testimony of a Master *is rejected by others of his time*. In Mark 6:4, it says: "And Jesus said unto them, 'A prophet is not without honor, save in his own country, and among his own kin, and in his own house.'" It wasn't only Jesus who was rejected. It happened to John and it happened to James.

Jesus, John 5:35: "'He was a burning and shining lamp, and you were willing to rejoice for a while in his light.'" How much interpreting is necessary for one to see that this is Jesus describing another Master? Is there some other plausible explanation for the rejoicing Jesus bothers to mention? Who else has "light" but a "Christ" (or "Master")? Jesus, John 5:36: "'But the testimony which I have is greater than that of John; for the works which the Father has granted me to accomplish, these very works which I am doing, bear me witness that the Father has sent me.'" Jesus was comparing himself with John, because John commanded such great respect among the people. His "works," however, were his "testimony." ("Works" will figure prominently at Qumran, later in this chapter.) Read John 1:1-13 again: "But to all who received him, who believed in his name [the Holy Spirit in John], he gave power to become children of God" (John 1:12). John says about Jesus, "'he who is coming after me is mightier than I, whose sandals I am not worthy to carry; he will baptize you with the Holy Spirit and with fire.'" (Matthew 3:11b-12). Matthew 11:11, 13-14: "'Truly, I say to you, among those born of women there has risen *no one* [including Jesus] greater than John the Baptist; yet he who is least in the kingdom of heaven is greater than he. For all the law and the prophets prophesied until John; and if you are willing to accept it, he is Elijah [another Master] who is to come [reincarnate—all Masters are One].'" How much higher praise can Jesus give John? Jesus didn't denigrate John. John did! He did so in order to deflect devotion from himself to Jesus, because he knew it is only natural for disciples to want to continue following a departing Master when a new one has come. As related above, that does not mean John had *any less power* to "baptize." These are *two Masters*, baptizing! He is asking the people present at the time *if they* are "willing to accept it." *Are we?*

The Dr. James Tabor website "A Hebrew Gospel of Matthew" (http://www.religiousstudies.uncc.edu/JDTABOR/shemtovweb.html) contains this discussion of what original Matthew contained regarding John the Baptist and what some key changes were in the received Matthew (verbatim):

> ST [Shem Tov Hebrew Matthew] never identifies Jesus as the Christ; e.g. 1:1 "these are the generations of Jesus . . ."; 1:18 "The birth of Jesus was in this way . . ." etc. John the Baptizer plays an exalted role: Matt. 11:11 "Truly, I say to you, among all those born of women [none] has risen greater than John the Baptizer." Phrase "yet he who is least in the kingdom of heaven is greater than he" is missing. In the Lucan parallel (7:28), mss. 5, 475 and 1080 also omit the qualification. The same reading is inferred in the Pseudo-Clementine Writings [Clement], Rec 1.60.1-3, where one of the disciples of John argues that his teacher is greater than Jesus, Moses,

and all men and thus the Christ. Also, in Rec 1.63.1 Peter taught the disciples of John not to allow John to be a stumbling-block to them. Matt. 11:13 "For all the prophets and the law spoke concerning [al] John" in contrast to the Greek: "For all the prophets and the law prophesied until John." Matt. 17:11 "Indeed Elijah will come and will save all the world" in contrast to the Greek: "Elijah does come, and he is to restore all things." Matt. 21:32 "Because John came to you in the way of righteousness and you did not believe him. But violent men and harlots believed him and you saw it and did not turn in repentance. Also afterward you did not repent to believe him. To the one who has ears to hear let him hear in disgrace." These words are directed *to his disciples* [italics mine] (v. 28), not to the chief priests and elders as in the Synoptic Greek tradition. The kind of polemic found in the Gospel of John appears to be directed toward an evaluation of John the Baptizer such as that found in Matthew. Similar reflective evidence is found in Luke-Acts and the Pseudo-Clementines (noted above).

Irenaeus, Adv. Haer. 3.1.1

"Matthew also issued a written Gospel among the Hebrews in their own dialect while Peter and Paul were preaching at Rome and laying the foundations of the church."

Origen (Eusebius, H.E. 6.25.4)

"As having learnt by tradition concerning the four Gospels, which alone are unquestionable in the Church of God under heaven, that first was written according to Matthew, who was once a tax collector but afterwards an apostle of Jesus Christ, who published it for those who from Judaism came to believe, composed as it was in the Hebrew language."

Eusebius, H.E. 3.24.6

"Matthew had first preached to Hebrews, and when he was on the point of going to others he transmitted in writing in his native language the Gospel according to himself, and thus supplied by writing the lack of his own presence to those from whom he was sent."

[George]Howard argues ["The Gospel of Matthew according to a primitive Hebrew Text"] that Shem Tov did not create the Hebrew Matthew himself (e.g., translating from the Latin) but had an existing Hebrew text to work with—as he sometimes comments on its scribal errors and strange readings. Matt. 11:11 is a good case in point, as the Greek, Latin, and all other Matthean witnesses contain the qualifying phrase: "nonetheless, the least in the Kingdom of heaven is greater than he." Shem Tov comments on the unique Hebrew version he is following, and how its lack of such a phrase implies that John is greater than Jesus. If he were translating from the Latin, Greek, or any other version such a comment would be meaningless.

Peter taught *the disciples* not to allow John to be a "stumbling block" to their belief in Jesus. Jesus taught them (*not* the chief priests and elders) that they should have "believed" John when he came to them in *the way of righteousness* (more on this language at Qumran later in the chapter). In the space of this short excerpt, Tabor cites at least a dozen ways John was minimized in favor of Jesus in Greek Matthew as compared to the earlier Hebrew. Someone was bent on marginalizing John the Baptist, a true Master.

For a more complete discussion of the origins of Matthew and Shem Tov's fourteenth century translation of, we can presume, the Hebrew version he claims to have used in his "Even Bochan", the reader can go to http://www.datingthenewtestament.com/Matthew.htm to get some idea of the issues involved and where we can see that even scholars become misled by orthodox assumptions such as John the Baptist's supposedly subordinate role in early Judaic Christian circles. John's lofty stature in the Hebrew Matthew and the lack of the "Trinity" doctrine in 28:19 coupled with the directive to preach to the gentiles are cited as *weaknesses* by many scholars *when they are actually reasons to be cited as supportive elements* for a Hebrew original, when the true teachings of John, Jesus, and James are correctly deduced.

Craig Davis, from his "Dating the New Testament" website:

> The Shem Tov Matthew has many examples of puns, alliteration and word connections, far more than in the Greek text of Matthew or even modern Hebrew texts that were translated from the Greek. These types of literary devices are common in Biblical Hebrew, but it is unlikely that Shem Tov created them, as he was

opposed to the Christian message and would not want to make the text more literary than it really was. It is also unlikely that this text was translated from Greek, as modern Hebrew translations of Matthew do not have many of these literary devices. The literary nature of the book indicates that its ancestral text, its original, may not have been a translation at all, but rather may have been originally written in Hebrew. In one example of word-play, the Hebrew of Matt. 10:36 says the "enemies" (oyevim) are to be "loved ones" (ohuvim). There are too many such examples to list. There is one very prominent play on words in the Greek text of Matthew, and it occurs in 16:18, where Jesus says to Peter, "you are Peter (Petros), and on this rock (petra) I will build my church." Interestingly, the Hebrew text of that verse contains a different play on words. Jesus says, "You are a stone (Eben), and upon you I will build (Ebenah) my house of prayer."

The genealogies in Matthew and Luke reveal a telling difference. Matthew uses the archaic Old Testament Hebrew language formula A begat B, B begat C, etc., but Luke's Greek is contemporary—B, son of A, C, son of B, etc. Also, Matthew 1:25, where Joseph "knew her not" (KJV) until Jesus was born alludes to a Hebrew origin for the term for marital relations, not Greek. Finally, consider this—a pun which materializes in Hebrew but is absent in the Greek: Matthew 7:6: "Do not throw your pearls before swine [*Hebrew chazir*], lest they trample them under foot and turn [yi**chazr**u] to attack you."

Much of the internal evidence in Matthew shows a message directed at a Judaic audience prior to the fall of the Temple in 70 CE. Since Jesus began his ministry preaching in Synagogues and to Jews like himself, Hebrew would have been Matthew's logical choice for the writing of this early gospel. While the Shem Tov Hebrew Matthew translation may not be a perfect text, it is substantially valid as representative of original Matthew in this writer's opinion, based on both the linguistic and internal evidence cited above—especially the direction of the theological changes evident when there is transition from the Hebrew version into the Greek—not vice versa—doctrinal and historical corruptions consistent with what we will soon find elsewhere in the New Testament.

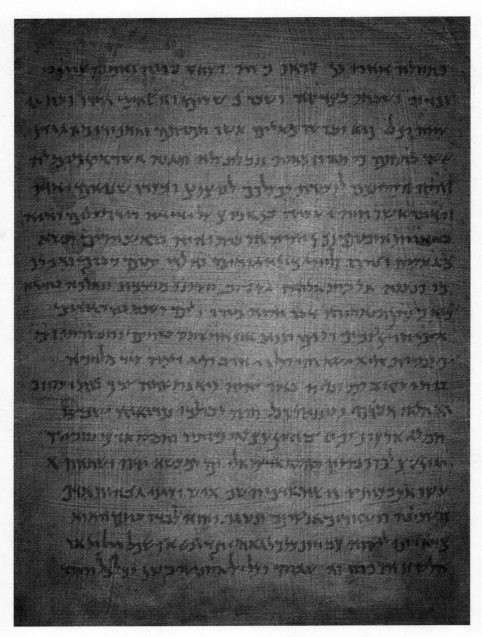

A sample of first-century Dead Sea Scroll material.

Caves where the Dead Sea Scrolls were discovered.

Dead Sea desert where the Qumran ruins are found.

The Dead Sea.

When John the Baptist "baptize[s] you with water for repentance" (Matthew 3:11a), John isn't talking about the river waters of the Jordan. This is a key oversight in Christian teaching. He means by "water," *allegorically*, the Holy Spirit! Check a Concordance to see how many times "water" or "waters" mean "spirit" in the Bible. "God made the firmament and separated the waters which were under the firmament from the *waters* which were *above the firmament*" in Genesis 1:7, "And God called the firmament *Heaven*" (v 1:8). The "water," then, is *above* Heaven as well as below it. So "water" for these people means *much more* than the splashy wet stuff. Early "Jewish Christian" groups or preChristian—Ebionites, Elchasites, Masbuthaeans, Arabic Sabaeans, Mandaeans, and even Essenes—all have in common "daily bathing" purification rituals, a preparation for entering into their particular spiritual practices, a part of "works righteousness." Large ritual baths are prominent even today in the ruins at Qumran.

James the Just

On Christmas Day, 1910, a front-page news story in the New York Times carried the explosive story of the discovery of an ancient manuscript, published by a Cambridge University scholar named Solomon Schechter, in a Cairo synagogue. Describing an ascetic community in the desert at a place identified as "Damascus," it became known as the Damascus Document. Multiple copies of the Damascus ("Zadokite") Document were among those uncovered in the Dead Sea Scrolls found later at Qumran, Jordan, in 1947. This manuscript, along with several others—the "Community Rule," the "Manual of Discipline," and the "Habakkuk Pesher"—outlining rules and beliefs for the desert "Ebionites"

(Ebionim, "The Poor" QpHab XII:3—"the poor" in Romans 15:26) as they are known from extra-biblical sources, became instrumental in reconstructing the First Century relationship of the Jerusalem Christians to the desert ascetic community. The original working group on the Scrolls, with strong ties to the Catholic Church, assigned a 200 BCE provenance to them, as a possible scriptorium for a sect of Essene monks, thus misleading everyone for some 30 years as to their true dating in the early Christian period. Of particular interest, aside from the discovery of a strict Torah-abiding Judaic Christian tone in the original "Jesus movement," was mention of three individuals with the cryptic titles of "The Righteous Teacher," the Spouter of Lying," and the "Wicked Priest." It was several more decades before Dr. Robert H. Eisenman put all the pieces together and revealed what appears to be their correct identifications. In his seminal work James, the Brother of Jesus is told, in exhaustive detail, the story of the writing out of the New Testament the central importance of James the Just, Jesus' brother, and as it turns out, spiritual heir. His more recent book, The New Testament Code, adds more detail and depth to the first work.

The Zadokites, or "Zaddikim," or "Sons of Zadok," encountered in Ezekiel 44 were identified in the Dead Sea Scroll's Damascus Document as "the elect of Israel" and in the Habakkuk Pesher (commentary on Habakkuk) as those who "would execute Judgment at the End of Time [*each one's time*, of course, not the world's!]." The terms are allied with the Hebrew concept of "Hesed" (Piety) and "Zedek" (Righteousness), the Holy Ones who would "justify the Righteous," such as the (mystic Jewish Kabbalah) Zohar's prototypical Zadok, Noah. Besides James, other Zadoks included second-century BCE Judas Maccabee (wilderness-dwelling vegetarian according to 2 Maccabees 5:27), Honi "the Circle Drawer" (so-named because he would not leave a circle drawn on the ground until God made it rain) and his grandson, Hanan "the Hidden"—none other than John the Baptist ("Hanan" in Hebrew comes from "Johanan" or "John"). According to Eisenman "Only an atonement by a *Righteous Priest/Zaddik* [italics original] could be considered *efficacious in terms of ultimate forgiveness for sin and entrance into the Messianic community/Kingdom of Heaven* [italics mine]." What we have now is a veritable full-on proliferation of Saviors! Melchizedek is an enigmatic figure, mentioned in both the Old (Gen. 14:18, "king" of Salem, "priest of God Most High", and Psalm 110:4, where David's king is a "priest forever according to the order of Melchizedek") and the New (Heb. 5-7) Testaments. "He is first, by translation of his name, king of *righteousness,* and then he is also king of Salem, that is, king of *peace.* He is without father or mother or genealogy, and has neither beginning nor end of life, but *resembling the Son of God* he continues a priest of God *forever*" (Heb. 7:2-3). This is obviously no ordinary "king"! In Genesis (14:20) none other than righteous Abraham is tithing to him. (And it isn't goods he was concerned with [v 23], Abraham was giving God a tenth of his *time* in devotions--the real meaning of "tithing"--to a "priest" of "God Most High", or, his "Master." No true Master accepts anything material from a disciple--*ever*.) This is born out in a Dead Sea Scroll fragment, "The Coming of Melchizedek" (11Q13, Col. 2 [http://www.gnosis.org/library/commelc.htm]), where "the Day of Atonement is the e[nd of the] tenth [Ju]bilee, when all the sons of [light] and the men of the lot of Mel[chi]zedek *will be atoned for*" (v 8, variant). Scroll 11Q13 has Melchizedek as the divine being (Col. 2, line 12) sitting in judgment in Psalms 7 (vv 7-8, "*The Lord* judges the peoples ...") and 82 (v 1, "*God* has taken his place in the divine councils"), whose *"feet"* bring "good tidings" (a mystic allusion to the inner Master) in Isaiah 52:7 (Col. 2, line 18), and proclaims "liberty to the captives" in Isaiah 61:1 (Col. 2, line 4 and line 17, "The visitation is *the Day of Salvation* [italics mine] that He has decreed through Isaiah the prophet"). Col. 2, line 26: "This scripture's interpretation: he is to instruct them about all the periods of history for eternity (... and in the statutes) of the truth. (...) (.... dominion) that passes from Belial [Satan] and returns to the Sons of Light (....) (...) by the judgment of God, just as [i]t is written concerning him; *who says to Zion 'Your divine being reigns'* (Isa. 52:7) *'Zion'* is the congregation of all the sons of righteousness, who uphold the covenant and turn from walking in the way of the people. *'Your divine being'* is Melchizedek, who will deliver them from the power of Belial. [italics original]" Called by God forty-two generations (Melchizedek was a contemporary of Abraham) *later,* Jesus Christ came *for his own "captives"* (Heb. 5:1-6) "after the order" of "priest" Melchizedek, Abraham's Master.

The Qumran discoveries, and details from the works of the historian Josephus made clear the details which would lead to Dr. Eisenman's identification of the Qumran Righteous Teacher as either James, or John and then James, and the "Wicked Priest" responsible for his death in 62 CE as High Priest Ananus ben Ananus, son of Ananus (Annas, Acts 4:6) which, according to Eisenman, is the immediate cause of the destruction of the Temple shortly thereafter (and *not* Jesus, as is commonly supposed).

James is identified as the Qumran Righteous Teacher by the recurrence of similar word types (hence, the "code") rooted, here, in the B-L-A letter family "Beliar," "Balaam," "Balak," "Diablos," "Beelzebub," "Babylon," and others, meaning "Devil" in both Greek and Hebrew usages that appear in both the New Testament in connection with the antagonist of James, and in the Dead Sea Scrolls in connection with the enemy of the Righteous Teacher. The real bombshell was the revealing of this individual as none other than New Testament megastar Paul as "the Liar." Eisenman relates that while the book of Acts—the Acts "of the Apostles"—is intended to cover what the Apostles did immediately after Christ left the earth, most are ignored in favor of extensive coverage of the doings of Paul, not an Apostle, "who, about a third of the way through the narrative, metamorphoses into its central focus and darling." If James became the leader of the Jerusalem church—the center of early Christendom—as the Qumran writings reveal, why is he virtually ignored? The "election" of an Apostle to replace Judas (Matthias, Acts 1:26) is a stand-in for the installation of James as leader of the church in Jerusalem, which would logically occur here and does not, the author wanting to avoid elevating anyone subsequent to Jesus who might be a rival to Paul, who fairly takes over the narrative by the middle of Acts. When Paul is seen giving greetings to the "family of Aristobulus" in Romans 16:10, including Salome, wife of Aristobulus (according to Josephus), whose "dance before King Herod Antipas" leads directly to John the Baptist's arrest and execution, it is clear Paul has connections which should raise eyebrows. This Matthew 14, Mark 6 "head on a platter" flourish is, according to Eisenman, an example of anti-Semitic pro-Roman, Hellenizing disinformation based perhaps on the Josephus account of Nero's wife Poppea asking for the head of *his former wife* "on a platter."

Details of the attack on James (and Paul's role in it) are key to unraveling what then happened in Acts. James was in fact so important a figure that his being the brother of Jesus is perhaps the only verifiable fact with which we can at all confirm the existence of the historical Jesus! With the primary account of this event from Eusebius, the preeminent early church historian, three separate notices are in evidence: one from each of Clement, Hegesippus, and Jerome—all extra-biblical sources. Additional information is gleaned from the so-called Pseudoclementines, novels of Peter's traveling companion, Clement, the Nag Hammadi books, and the Dead Sea Scrolls. In chapter 7 of Acts, showing that the stoning of Stephen (the Greek-derived "stephen" means "crown"—a reference to the long hair worn by the Nazarites, a sect associated with James, as well as Samson [Hebrew, "like the sun"] of Samson and Delilah fame, and the origin of the Jesus "of Nazareth" myth) in Acts is actually a stand-in for an attack on James by Paul in the Hegesippus account of it, where James—not Jesus—utters the famous "Father forgive them for they know not what they do." Eisenman traces the parallel references of the attack on James by Paul and his supporters who break one or both of his legs (he "limps" on in it later in Clement's Pseudoclementines) in the Acts cover story, and after being taken to "the house of James" as per the Latin version of the Pseudoclementines (which shows up in both the Acts 12:12 story of "Peter" miraculously going to the house of Mary, mother of "John Mark," where "they were praying" [over grievously injured James], and also the crucifixion scenario of John and Mary being united as mother and son) and what would happen to the perpetrator (the "Wicked Priest" Ananus) of the second, fatal, attack on the Righteous Teacher in the Scroll's Habakkuk Pesher. Both sources drawing on Isaiah 3:9-11, the language of "swallowing" or "eating the fruit of their doings" is associated with James the Just, as shown in a verbatim account from Eusebius of Hegesippus' version of the Isaiah passage: "Let us take away the Just One, for he is abhorrent to us, wherefore they shall eat of the fruit of their doings" instead of the received version: "Say to the Righteous, all is well, for they [the Evil] shall eat of the fruit of their doings." Either Hegesippus' Greek Septuagint version or the received version is tampered with. While there is a clear case to be made for the latter, in whatever case, an ancient authority has James as the subject of the evil "eating the fruit of their doings" which appears in both the Jamesian Jerusalem Community tradition and the Qumran Community tradition: "Woe to the wicked. It shall be ill with him, for the Reward of his hands will be done to him." (v 3:11). The same word "Reward" or "Gamul" is used in the Habakkuk Pesher concerning the "Wicked Priest" who "plotted to destroy the poor" and his assassination, where it is said "the Reward which he paid the Poor [Jamesian Ebionites in Jerusalem] would be paid to him." Eisenman concludes here "Since the material about the Wicked Priest 'being paid the Reward he paid' others from Isaiah 3:10-11 nowhere appears in the materials from Habakkuk under consideration, it is clear that the writers at Qumran knew this material from Isaiah 3:10-11 and were incorporating it into their presentation of the death of their 'Righteous Teacher.'" Hence, the connection between the Qumran Community's "Righteous Teacher" of the Habakkuk Pesher with the Acts 7:52 reference to the killing of the prophesied "Just [or

'Righteous'] One," meant here, of course, to apply to Jesus—but in reality, as per Hegesippus, applies to James.

Really, the simple thrust of the new information on Paul points to the heart of New Testament dynamics. Not universally recognized before, the theme of "righteousness by faith" of Paul in his letters is set at counterpoint to the real teachings of James and Jesus, as evidenced in the letter of James and some of Jesus' discourses. Habakkuk 2:4 "the righteous shall live by his faith" becomes for Paul "Now it is evident that no man is justified before God by law, for 'He who through faith is righteous *shall live*' " (Gal. 3:11, RSV). Big difference! Change the word order slightly and the emphasis of the sentence shifts from living (works righteousness of James) to the faith justified righteousness doctrine of Paul: "through faith [he] *is* righteous." Genesis 15:6, Abraham saying "And he believed the Lord; and he reckoned it [his God-blessed progeny] to him as righteousness" is used by Paul to support his faith-righteousness doctrine. Small problem, though: The "he" in "he reckoned" is ~~God—not~~ Abraham. It isn't present in the Hebrew and when that is the case, the understood pronoun refers to the subject of the prior clause: Abraham. The ~~KJV~~ YCT plays into the error by capitalizing it (perhaps knowingly)! Paul, reading from the Greek Septuagint, was sucked in. The Hebrew for "righteousness" is "sedaqa"—also meaning "justice." Thus, in the Hebrew original of the verse, Abraham is counting the promise of God as *justice to himself,* not as God's *justification* of him. This subtle commandeering of a basic precept, co-opting it into something entirely new is a hallmark of Paul's, and he well knew his craft. Consider this far-fetched argument: "Therefore, if food is the cause of my brother's falling, I will never eat meat, lest I cause my brother to fall" (1 Cor. 8:13). "All things are lawful," but not all things are helpful" (v 10:23a). "Eat whatever is sold in the meat market without raising question on grounds of conscience." (v 25). "For the earth is the Lord's, and everything in it" (v 26, quoting the first line of Psalm 24). Talk about a reach! Eisenman: "These are perhaps some of the most cynical and manipulative rhetorical displays in the disappointing history of theological dialectic." Eisenman's The Dead Sea Scrolls and the First Christians, James, the Brother of Jesus and The New Testament Code plumb thoroughly the depths of Paul's imaginings and it isn't possible to pursue it all here. With literally *thousands* of items which cross-check with historians Flavius Josephus, Hegesippus, Eusebius, Epiphanius and Jerome, as well as newly discovered texts from the 1947 Dead Sea Scrolls discoveries at Qumran in showing that details of the life of James have been co-opted into the lives of other figures in the New Testament Book of Acts and the Gospels, a picture of almost unimaginable intrigue and deception emerges. This manipulation, overwriting, and suppression has been done purposefully by Paul, the writer of the Gospel of Luke, the writer of Acts (with "its clearly evasive and/or misleading thrust"), and to a lesser degree by Matthew, Mark, Josephus, and perhaps even Jerome, church historian. In his groundbreaking presentation Eisenman masterfully searches the historical record for telltale signs of the true history of the time of Jesus. Our understanding of the roles of central players such as James, Paul, Herod and Ananus is forever changed. Obviously, the implications for Christianity are enormous. The debate over these identities and the person of the historic Jesus Christ is fully engaged at the present time with the discovery of these amazing time-machine documents at Qumran's ruins.

For example, paraphrasing Eisenman from footnote 146, Chapter 1, in The Dead Sea Scrolls and the First Christians we begin to see the magnitude of obfuscation: The problem of Jesus' brothers bedevils Apostle lists and post-resurrection appearances. Josephus calls Theudas a "magician." Like "Judas Thomas," he is a Joshua redivivus, or Jesus "lookalike." His relationship with "Addai" (cf. elsewhere "Thaddeus," or "Judas the Zealot," or even "Judas Iscariot") and with Jesus' family is signaled at Nag Hammadi ("Theuda the father of the Just One"—read "brother of"—2 Apoc. Jas. 5:44, for "Addai," see 1 Apoc. Jas. 5:36). The additional phrase found there, "since he was a relative of his," shows the way towards sorting out all these confusing references to "brothers," sons," and "fathers." What Acts has done is substitute the beheading of "James *the brother of John*" for Theudas/Thaddeus/Judas (also Lebbaeus, "of James," and probably Judas *Thomas) the brother of Jesus.* Note that it is the "brother" theme which is constant. The fictional "John and James *the sons of Zebedee"* is part of the process of downplaying and eliminating Jesus' brothers (and successors in Palestine) from scripture. The Central Triad of the early Jerusalem Church can now be identified as James (the brother of Jesus), Cephus (Peter), and John of Galations 2:9, not the misleading "Peter, James, and John *his brother"* of the Gospels. The nonsense of Mary, *"the sister of* mother Mary, wife of Clophas [Cleophas]" (John 19:25), "the mother of James and Joses [Jesus] and the mother of the sons of Zebedee" (Matthew 27:56), of "James the less [more nonsense], Joses, and Salome" (Mark 15:40), and of "James" (Luke 24:10), disappears and now becomes simply *Jesus' mother.* Papias fragment 10 in the Ante-Nicene Fathers identifies Thaddeus as the son of Mary and Cleophas (the Gospels' Joseph) and the brother of James, Simon (Simeon), and Joses. Complicit in the attack on truth, church Fathers Origen and Eusebius are willing to call James "the brother of Jesus" even though of different fathers *and* mothers. There is no way to cover here in any comprehensive way the breadth of this examination, so the reader is referred to the Eisenman work in the most emphatic way possible for a guide to sorting out the incredibly complex weaving of altered identities, multiple names, purposeful obfuscations, outright lies, rewrites and juxtapositions of major events and characters, and just general mayhem on the proper understanding of what happened in the tumultuous time of Roman occupied Palestine.

The conclusion Dr. Eisenman reaches can be summed up in his final sentence: "Who and whatever James was, so was Jesus." "Once James has been rescued from the oblivion into which he was cast, abetted by one of the most successful rewrite enterprises ever accomplished—the Book of Acts (and one of the most fantastic)—it is necessary to deal with the new constellation of facts the reality of his being occasions. *It will no longer be possible to avoid, through endless scholarly debate and other evasion syndromes, the obvious solution to the problem of the Historical Jesus*—the question of his actual physical existence aside—the answer to which is simple. *Who and whatever James was, so was Jesus* [italics mine]." For the first time in history, we now have a recognized scholar revealing the stupendous truth of *the real Gospel.* Jesus was not alone as Savior. Eisenman didn't *say* so, but now he can. Perhaps the Gospel of Thomas (often regarded as the "fifth Gospel" and with origins perhaps earlier even than the canonical ones as it is a "sayings" record) tells it best (12b): "[Jesus Christ]: 'In the place where you [disciples] are to go [probably Jerusalem], go to James the Just *for whose sake heaven and earth have come into existence.*'" If this passage doesn't put James on par with Jesus Christ, one should perhaps read it again. In writing this book, this writer originally called in conclusion for a systematic survey of the scriptures for evidence of the writing out of history of evidence of other Masters besides Jesus, *not aware that it had already been done*, albeit presumably without the author's recognition of having done so. The present work is the only addition necessary to what Dr. Eisenman has achieved to establish—once and for all—the existence in biblical scripture of other Masters besides Jesus Christ. This book shows *the significance* of what happened. Eisenman shows *how* it happened. Read together, the conclusion *is unassailable*. Paul was determined to eliminate and erase James as Jesus' rightful heir and successor as Master in his own right, and establish his own church and doctrine. He succeeded. That is, until now.

The discovery in 1945 in the Egyptian desert of another set of ancient manuscripts, only recently presented to the public (1978)—the treasures at Nag Hammadi, including, among many others, The Apocryphon of James and two others known as The First Apocalypse of James and The Second Apocalypse of James—made it even clearer that the Righteous Teacher was none other than James. In The Apocryphon of James (15:30) written to "a minister of the salvation of the saints"—perhaps the heterodox teacher Cerinthus—James tells the other disciples what the Lord Jesus has revealed in a vision to Peter and himself. "'[Disciples to Peter and James:] What did you hear from the Master? And what has he said to you? And where did he go?' But we [Peter and James] answered them, "He has ascended and has given us a pledge and promised life to us all and revealed to us children who are come after us, after bidding us love them, *as we would be [saved] for their sakes.* "And when they heard (this), they indeed believed the revelation, but were displeased about those to be born. And so, not wishing to give them offense, I sent each one to another place. But I myself went up to Jerusalem, praying that I might *obtain a portion among the beloved,* who will be made manifest. And I pray that the beginning may come from you, for *thus I shall be capable of salvation, since they will be enlightened through me,* by my faith—and through another (faith) that is better than mine [Jesus'], for I would that mine be the lesser. Endeavor earnestly, then, to make yourself like them and pray that you might obtain a portion with them. For because of what I have said, the savior did not make the revelation to us for their sakes. We do, indeed, proclaim a portion *with those for whom the proclamation was made, those the Lord has made his sons.*'" This is James describing Jesus' commission to him and Peter to initiate ("proclaim a portion with") "those the Lord has made his sons." The power of Jesus ("another faith that is better than mine") was to work *through them,* just as John the Baptist's power worked through Jesus (Matthew 3:13-17). The Nag Hammadi Apocalypses of James (both First and Second) support the portrait of James as successor Master to Jesus. From the Second Apocalypse of James 55:1-22: "[I—James] wish to reveal through you and the [Spirit of Power], in order to reveal *[to those] who are yours.* And those who wish to enter, and who seek to walk in the way that is before the door, *open the good door THROUGH YOU.* And they follow you; they enter [and you] escort them inside, and give a reward to each one who is ready for it. For you are not the redeemer nor a helper *of strangers.* You are an illuminator and a redeemer [Master] of those who are mine, and now *of those who are yours*. You shall reveal (to them); you shall bring good among them all." No guessing here. That is a risen Master describing the salvation of souls by a successor Master. They are not *strangers* because the predecessor *marked them* for his successor. Introduced by Charles W. Hedrick in James M. Robinson's The Nag Hammadi Library, this book is early: "Because of the basic Jewish-Christian traditions out of which the tractate is composed, it is probable that its origin is to be associated with Jewish-Christian circles [Jerusalem or Qumran—Jamesian not Pauline]. The absence of allusions to the later developed gnostic systems, and the almost total absence of allusions to the New Testament tradition suggest an early date for the origin of the tractate [probably 60's CE]."

The fictional election of Matthias where should be the election or appointment of James as successor to Jesus and the stoning of Stephen where James is attacked by Paul in other more historical sources are only two of the incredible number of details Eisenman brings out to show the overwriting of, or ignoring of, James' central role in the early church with fictions meant to marginalize the whole family of Jesus and aggrandize Paul in his stead. Paul's many references to "not lying," and conspicuous use of "righteous man" terminology, his employment of his "justification by faith" ruse in contradistinction to Jamesian "justification by works *and* faith" doctrine (see the letter of James), and derogatory treatment of Peter (continually needing three visions in Acts to get the message of "clean"—as if he never had the chance to hear it from Jesus all those years with him!—and needing to hear Jesus tell him to "feed my sheep"—*three* times, denying the Lord—*three* times—etc.) in the Gospels and Acts are obvious reactionary defensive measures employed by Paul and his apologists to justify his maneuverings into early church leadership from a position of universal rejection—even excommunication—by "fellow" Apostles. By the end of Acts none of them wanted anything to do with him. The "Righteous Teacher" of Qumran and Jerusalem in the Dead Sea Scrolls is James. His nemesis, "the Liar" ("Lying Spouter," or "Scoffer"), is Paul. "The Cup of the Lord" which James drinks in his last encounter with Jesus in the Gospel of the Hebrews (an apocryphal book) is both the assumption of Mastership and the acceptance of their shared fate. The "Cup of the New Covenant in my blood" that Paul works into his idea of blood atonement in 1 Corinthians 11:25 is a warping of the "New Covenant in the Land of Damascus" in the Habakkuk Pesher and Damascus Document of the Dead Sea Scrolls, "Damascus" translating from the Hebrew "Dammashek" and the Greek "dam" for "blood" and "chos" for "cup" in a turnaround play on a fundamental teaching at the Jamesian Qumran community, "abstaining from blood" sacrificial offering and even meat-eating (Jamesian Christians were vegetarians) into the Pauline creation of Christian "blood-sacrifice" through crucifixion of Christ—*never taught by Jesus Christ.* The "belligerence" as Eisenman puts it, of Paul towards his enemies (mainly James and his Jerusalem followers) with regard to "drinking Judgment unto oneself" (1 Cor. 11:29) is an attempt by Paul to deflect the condemnations *of himself* as "the Spouter of Lying" in the Dead Sea Scroll's Habakkuk Pesher, X:6-13: "Woe unto him who builds a City on Blood and establishes a township on Unrighteousness. Behold, does this not come from the Lord of Hosts, that the Peoples labor for the sake of Fire and the Peoples tire themselves out for the sake of Nothingness [Hab. 2:12-13]? The interpretation of the passage is about the Spouter of Lying, who leads many astray, in order to build a Worthless City upon Blood and erect an Assembly [or 'Church'] upon Lying, for the sake of his Glory, tiring out the Many with a Worthless Service and instructing them in works of Lying, so that their 'amal' ['suffering works'] will be of Emptiness [cf. 'Empty Man' allusion, James 2:20]. And they will be brought to the (same) Judgments of Fire, with which they insulted [or 'blasphemed'] and vilified the Elect of God." One way to establish the identity of the "Liar" as Paul, aside from the "blood" argument with James here, is to turn to Romans 3:7 and 9:1, 2 Corinthians 11:31, Galations 1:20, and 1 Timothy 2:7 to see how defensive Paul was about accusations of "lying" from the Jamesians. Then James 2:14 and 3:14, 1 John 1:6, 1:10, 2:4, 2:21ff., 4:20, 5:10, and Revelation 2:2 and 2:14 show other New Testament authors were aware of the situation created by Paul's teachings and the "lying" language appertaining to it—Jude 18 even using the Dead Sea Scroll's "scoffer" moniker. Further confirmation is Habakkuk Pesher Column II:1-8: "(Its interpretation [of Habakkuk's vision in Hab. 1:5] concerns) the Traitors with the Man of Lying, because he did not (believe what the) Righteous Teacher expounded from the mouth of God. (And it concerns) the Trai(tors to the Laws of God and the New Covenant [Paul's followers]), since they did not believe in the Covenant of God (and defiled His) Holy Name [the 'Word'—chapter two]. Likewise the interpretation of the passage (concerns the Trai)tors to the Last Days. These are the Vio(lent Ones and the Covenant-Brea)kers, who did not believe all that they heard was (going to happen to) the Last Generation from the mouth of the Priest [James], (in whose heart) God put (the intelligence) to interpret all the words of

His Servants the Prophets, (through whom) God foretold all that was coming to His People." Column VI:4 date stamps the Pesher as unfolding in the first century CE—not before, in perhaps the Maccabean period as some have suggested—since the "Kittim," or Romans "sacrifice to their standards [banners] and worhip their weapons of war," as was done by Imperial legions, not BCE Republican troops. With this understanding, and the context of the commentary paralleling Paul's letters concerning what was then going on between him and James, the only one the "Man of Lying" here can possibly be is Paul. It cannot be overly stressed the vital importance of this recently discovered document. What does this not say of the viability of the Christian Faith? Here we have the author of the central Christian teaching of blood salvation and righteousness by faith being called by the brother of Jesus—his acknowledged successor—the builder of an unrighteous fantasyland! There was no more pious, devout group allied with Jesus and James in the first century. The Zealot Ebionites at Jerusalem and Qumran were so devoted to their beliefs that when the Romans under Pompey besieged the Temple in 63 BCE they would not "blaspheme the Lawgiver" or consume "things sacrificed to idols"—not ceasing from their appointed religious duties even while being cut down with the sword (per Josephus and Hippolytus)! A whole community at Masada chose suicide to capitulation. These are a people who took their faith seriously.

At Qumran, according to the Ebionite and Elchasite ideology the righteous were known as "Sons of Zadok" or "Zaddiks" and would be "*standing* at the End Time," as we saw above, meaning of course, the end of life, not the end of the world.

"Standing" and "casting" word-form usage appears over and over in both New Testament and Qumran scripture and act as a kind of "code"—useful in identifying motives behind phrasing of many passages. "Standing" and "Standing One" refer to the righteous—Masters or their initiates—the unrighteous "Evil Ones" or "Traitors with the Man of Lying" (Habakkuk Pesher) are unworthy and "cast down." You will find these throughout the Dead Sea Scroll scriptures, Nag Hammadi texts as well as the New Testament: "There be some 'standing' here who will not taste death" (Matthew 16:28a, also, Matthew 12:46, Luke 24:36, John 20:14, 19, 26, and 21:4, Acts 1:10, and 7:55-6) "And he healed many who were sick, and 'cast out' many demons" (Mark 1:34, John 12:31, etc.). In the parable of the "poor widow" (Mark 12:41-45) "casting" appears *seven* times in four lines, and serves to connect the Gospels to the Dead Sea Scrolls' reference to "casting" the "Three Nets of Belial"—riches, fornication (niece marriage), and pollution of the "Temple" (CD IV:14-18, cf. Isaiah 24:17). Even more significantly, scribes thought *to remove* in translation the many references to "standing" from the original Hebrew Matthew—perhaps because they realized (were told?) the overt Jamesian Qumran connection and were attempting to protect Jesus' preeminence: "Standing" removed from text or altered to another verb (Shem Tov Hebrew Matthew): Matt. 26:69a, 69b, 71a, 71b, 73; 27:11, 47, 54, 55, 63, 64; 28:2, 4, 6, 7, and 8—in all, 16 occasions! Phrasing with these key words identifies parallel or identical figures of varying names or pseudonyms from one source to another, canonical with noncanonical, or from either with purely historical accounts.

Jesus' apocalyptic accounts in Matthew 24, Mark 13, and Revelation 12 and 13, as well as the Daniel 9 "Seventy-weeks prophecy" are all warnings of the first century siege and destruction of Jerusalem, not a prediction of world destruction in our time. The "lightning" coming from "east as far as west" and the sun and moon being darkened, with "the Son coming on the clouds of heaven" in Matthew are all inner spiritual experiences of a personal nature explored in depth in the next chapter. In these accounts, Jerusalem will be utterly destroyed by the Romans as Jesus foretold. Both Mark and Luke also say these things will happen (Mark 13:2, Luke 21:6). Nero is the "Beast" (666 or, in Latin, 616) of Revelation 13 persecuting "the woman" or loyal followers of James. "Seventy weeks of years" in Daniel 9:24-27 passed from the return from Babylonian captivity to the 69 CE siege of Jerusalem, and a "62-week" rebuilding of the Temple. The "people of the prince" come to destroy the city are the Roman legions of the coming "world ruler" Vespasian. The "anointed one" who is "cut off" after sixty-two weeks (seven years short of the siege) is James (the "male child caught up to God" (Rev. 12:5) after being slain by the "dragon" (the Devil, in Ananus). For "half a week" the ruler will cease Temple sacrifice and offerings, which Eisenman says is the final cause leading to the Roman attack. The "time, times, and half a time" is the three and a half year flight into the wilderness ("the Pella flight") on the two wings of the "great eagle" (Rev. 12:14) who is perhaps Simeon bar Cleophas (from Josephus). So none of this is pertinent to our time.

What soon becomes clear is a picture that will begin the inevitable rewriting of Christianity. The whole book of Acts, sadly, is from beginning to end a work of not just fiction, but fiction with a mission: a devious attempt by Luke to manipulate history into a self-serving portrayal of Paul at the expense of James, who should be the central character of the work. Before his stoning, the speech Stephen makes to the council in answer to the high priest's question about whether accusations he spoke "against this holy place and the law" (Acts 6:13) were true reveals an amazingly brazen example of this fiction. The entire thing, consuming the first 50 lines of Acts chapter 7, is a redivivus of Joshua's farewell speech in Joshua chapter 24. So faithful is the rendition that it even includes a mistake copied from the original! Jacob died, "himself and our fathers, and they were carried back to Shechem and laid in the tomb that Abraham had bought for a sum of silver from the sons of Hamor in Shechem" (Acts 7:15-16). Unfortunately for Luke, according to Genesis chapter 23 these ancestors were not buried at Shechem, but Machpelah, "east of Mamre, bought from Ephron the Hittite" (v 23:11). Actually, "The bones of Joseph which the people of Israel brought up from Egypt were buried at Shechem, in the portion of ground which Jacob bought from the sons of Hamor the father of Shechem for a hundred pieces of money, it became an inheritance of the descendants of Joseph." (Josh. 24:32). Somebody goofed when transcribing from Joshua, providing the proof as to where this speech originated. The absurdity of a Gentile lecturing to Jews about their own history (erroneously, at that!) closes with Stephen evoking "the coming of the Righteous One, whom you [Jews] have now betrayed and murdered." (Acts 7:52). As Eisenman points out, not only is this cognomen associated with James in Qumran literature, this line parallels James 5:6: "You have condemned; you have killed the righteous man; he does not resist you." "There, it will be recalled, not only did it precede the allusion to 'the coming of the Lord' and 'the Judge *standing* before the gate' (Jas. 5:8-9), but it was directed at "the Rich," (v 5:1), not against fictitious "Stephen's" Jews! The clothing placed at the feet of "a young man named Saul" (Acts 7:58) and Saul "consenting to his death" (v 8:1) both implicate Paul in the death of James—the real subject of the attack here. The clothing is not "'their' garments" but *James'* as the condemned is buried to the waist before stoning. This is clearly a link of responsibility to Paul. After speaking his piece, "Stephen" is then treated to a vision of the risen Lord Jesus, and "the Heavens opening and the Son of Man standing at the right hand of God" (vv 7:55-56) paralleled in the writings of Qumran regarding the Righteous Teacher, concluding with the plea "do not hold this sin against them" (v 7:60) which, of course, was similarly uttered by Jesus on the cross, but was really original with Qumran's Righteous Teacher, *both* applied in hindsight in the Gospels to Jesus. The Gospels' charge against Jesus for "blasphemy" of Matthew 26:63 and Mark 14:61 by the High Priest identifying him as "the Christ" and "the Son of God" (things Jesus himself never said, as we will see later) is likewise applied to Jesus retrospectively from the life of James as recounted by Jerome on the basis of Clement of Alexandria, according to Eisenman.

In the Dead Sea Scrolls, "Pentecost" is an annual reunion in the desert of the wilderness camps at "Damascus" (Qumran). This is the festival in Jerusalem that Paul is seen hurrying back to Jerusalem for in Acts 20:16 with funds he has collected overseas (cf. 2 Cor. 1:15-19, 8:13-9:15, Phil. 4:15-19). In Acts 21:24, James directs Paul on living in "observance of the law." This same phrasing is to be found in the last column of the Damascus

Document at Qumran *as a total rededication to the Law* and *"not deviating to the right or to the left of the Torah."* In calling for a separation of the faithful in the camps from backsliders like Paul's followers in Jerusalem, colorful imagery is evoked including "they pollute their Holy Spirit and open their mouth with *a Tongue* full of insults against the Laws of the Covenant of God" and "works of Abomination in a spirit of fornication and Ways of uncleanness in the service of pollution, *a Tongue* full of blasphemies" (Damascus Document V:12 and Community Rule IV:11). When coupled with how Paul is described as "Lying Spouter" and "Windbag" *"walking in windiness"* (Damascus Document) these word pictures slide easily into the Acts 2:1-6 rendition of the Holy Spirit as "mighty rushing wind" and the faithful "speaking with other tongues" betraying their likely origins—an attempt to counter an indictment of Paul from the Jamesians at Qumran with a thinly veiled reference to Micah 2:11: "If a man should go about and utter wind and lies, saying, 'I will preach to you of wine and strong drink,' he would be the preacher for this people!'" The circle of incrimination draws ever tighter around Paul.

Bishop John Shelby Spong gives a rather insightful reason for the animosity Paul felt towards the Jamesian law-abiding Jerusalem converts. He suggests Paul was a closet homosexual. The evidence is certainly worth considering. Although there is a slowly advancing acceptance of homosexuality today by the church, with more enlightened views of the nature of it and acknowledgment of its natural prevalence in the animal world, in the preChristian era things weren't so benign. Being expert in the Torah as he was, Paul was well aware of the Judaic proscription of homosexuality. His religious tradition would "clearly regard gay males as aberrant, distorted, evil, and depraved" as Bishop Spong writes in Rescuing the Bible from Fundamentalism: "When discovered, gay males were quite often executed. The law stated: 'You shall not lie with a man as with a woman; it is an abomination' (Lev. 18:22). 'If a man lies with a man as with a woman, both of them have committed an abomination; they shall be put to death'" (Lev. 20:13). For Paul, the flesh was the proving ground for mankind. The flesh produced "fornication, impurity, licentiousness" (Gal. 5:23). "Those who belong to Christ Jesus have *crucified the flesh* with its passions and desires" (Gal. 5:24). Again and again he warns, "Do not use your freedom as an opportunity for the flesh" (Gal. 5:13). "Do not gratify the desires of the flesh. For the desires of the flesh are against the Spirit, and the desires of the Spirit are against the flesh" (Gal. 5:16). Paul himself felt bedeviled by this human weakness: "For I do not do what I want, but I do the very thing that I hate" (Rom. 7:15). "Wretched man that I am! Who will deliver me from this body of death?" (Rom. 7:24). But he believed in marriage. "For it is better to marry than to be aflame with passion" (1 Cor. 7:9). So why the self-loathing? To the Galations: "You know it was because of a bodily ailment that I preached the gospel to you at first; and though my condition was a trial to you, you did not scorn or despise me but received me as an angel of God, as Christ Jesus." (Gal. 4:13). Paul told them he had now "become as they are," one in whom "Christ has been formed," and assured them that they "did him no wrong" (Gal. 4:12, 19). This refers to an inner not an external healing, so the flaw is one or orientation, not body. The clincher is 2 Corinthians.12:7-9: "And to help me keep from being too elated by the abundance of revelation, a thorn was given me in the flesh, a messenger of Satan, to harass me, to keep me from being too elated. Three times [*three*, again!] I sought the Lord about this, that it should leave me; but he said to me 'My grace is sufficient for you, for my power is made perfect in weakness.'" What "thorn" in the body was it that marriage would not cure which caused him such anguish as he sought to lead the new church? He must have been a gay man, doing "the very thing that I hate." He would certainly have felt threatened by a strict adherence to the Judaic laws which were so central to the Jamesian Christians, as compared to his more liberated "salvation grace through faith" doctrine. Here is the possible motive for the deep hatred Paul felt towards James and Peter that Eisenman so ably details.

Even stronger indictment of Paul came from Jesus himself. In Douglas Del Tondo's Jesus' Words Only, Paul finally gets his comeuppance at the hands of his beloved risen Lord Jesus himself in the revelation to John. ["To the angel of the church in Ephesus, write:] 'I know your works, your toil and your patient endurance, and how you cannot bear evil men but have tested *those who call themselves apostles but are not, and found them to be false*'" (Rev. 2:1-2). Ephesus is the only one of the seven "churches" in John's vision that was known to have been told by Paul that he was "an apostle" (Eph. 1:1). Jesus: "'But I have a few things against you: you have some there who hold the teaching of Balaam, who taught Balak [both B-L-A code words for "Devil" from the original] to put a stumbling block before the sons of Israel, *that you might eat food sacrificed to idols* and practice immorality'" (Rev. 2:14). Balaam is an Old Testament figure used in the Qumran texts as a representation of the embodiment of Satan, here applied to Paul who not only put *stumbling blocks* before the elect by telling the Corinthians, for example, 1 Corinthians 10:23, 25: "All things are lawful" and to eat "whatever is sold in the meat market without raising question on the grounds of conscience" but who also—in case anyone doubts the connection to Balaam (Num. 22:31)—*fell to the ground* (Acts 9:4) when the Lord suddenly appeared to him, as Paul, of course, does in his famous conversion episode on the road to "Damascus" (really Qumran!). Del Tondo shows Jesus is the only "inspired" source for what exactly Balaam's transgression was (Rev. 2:14) that led to his slaying by the Israelites in Numbers 31:8, unspecified in the condemnation of Balaam in 31:16 for bringing "plague among the congregation." In the Qumran Damascus Document it is Belial ("Devil" code again) who "casts" his "Three Nets" of fornication, Riches, and pollution of the Temple (outwardly the building, *inwardly* the consumption of forbidden food and drink). The Gospels point up this kind of asceticism when they describe John the Baptist as "coming neither eating or drinking"—this as opposed to the Paulinized description (remember—his letters came first) of Jesus coming "eating and drinking" (Matthew 11:18-19 and Luke 7:33-34) and reinforced by depictions of Jesus as a "glutton," "wine-bibber," (same verses) or "eating and drinking with publicans and sinners" (Luke 15:1-2) to try to make the point (wrongly) that he was not an ascetic Nazarite or "Nazoraean" but a "Nazarene" from somewhere called "Nazareth" (code word letters N-Z-R as in "lehinnazer"—Hebrew for "keep away" or "abstain from"). The Pauline denigrating of Jesus' family spared not even Jesus himself!

Del Tondo shows also Paul failing the test of a true prophet when he transgresses the law: "'You shall not add to the word which I command you nor take from it; that you may keep the commandments of the Lord your God which I have commanded you'" (Deut. 4:2), and "'If a prophet arises among you, or a dreamer of dreams, and gives you a sign or wonder which he tells you comes to pass, and if he says "Let us go after other gods," which you have not known, "and let us serve them," you shall not listen to the words of that prophet or to that dreamer of dreams'" (Deut. 13:1-30). And Jesus isn't the only condemnation we find of Paul in the scriptures. Paul's "cursing" ("anathema") of others who teach a gospel other than his (Gal. 1:8,9) or don't love Jesus (1 Cor. 16:22) is countermanded by James himself in James 3:10: "From the same mouth come blessing and cursing. My brethren, this ought not to be so" and Numbers 23:8: "How can I curse whom God has not cursed?" Calling others foolish: "'[whoever says] "You fool!" shall be liable to the hell of fire'" (Matthew 5:22). Boasting (2 Cor. 11:16, 17, 18, "I too may boast a little", "I say not with the Lord's authority, but as a fool, in this boastful confidence", "since many boast of worldly things, I too will boast"): "But he gives more grace; therefore it says, 'God opposes the proud, but gives grace to the humble'" (James 4:16). And judging others (Gal. 2:11-21, Paul turning around the whole teaching of Jesus and obedience to the Law into a condemnation of Peter): "'Judge not, that you be not judged'" (Matthew 7:1). Del Tondo goes on to show how Paul *negates* the Law in 1 Corinthians 9:20-21: "To the Jews I became as a Jew, in order to win Jews; to those under the law I became as one under the law—*though not being myself under the law*—that I might win those under the law. To those outside the law I became as one outside the law—not being without law toward God but under the law of Christ—that I might win those outside the law." "Me on autos hupo numon" is the Greek for the above italicized phrase. "Me" is *"not"*, meaning Paul is putting himself above the Law and outside the bounds of Christ's clear message earlier as found in the Gospels. This is the beginning of the permissive Pauline interpretation of the gospel message, and goes directly against the true teachings of the Law (Torah)-abiding Jesus, and of the tests of Deuteronomy 12, 13, and 18 for claims of prophetic authority. Jesus himself warned against such false teachers (Matthew 7:15, 24:11, 24, and Rev. 2:2 and 14), and of those especially who would *come in his name* (Mark 13:22-23). Del Tondo: "If these tests are to be ignored as to Paul in particular, *why do you think a decade prior to Paul's entry into Christian circles that Jesus emphasized repeatedly that false prophets were to to come?* [italics his] " He was speaking about Paul! Just because somebody put Paul's letters in the Bible doesn't mean they belong there. Scripture demands additions or changes to scripture be *tested by scripture.* Jesus' Words Only is one book that Paul will not survive. Douglas Del Tondo has emphatically and forever rewritten his place in history.

The need for expert guidance in exegesis of the Bible is illustrated in Matthew 4:12-16. Dr. Eisenman points out that the "Galilee of the Gentiles" (NRSV) in verse 15 isn't referring to the Sea of Galilee, or the area around it, but to "the Region" or "the Circle of the Gentiles" ("Galil" means "circle" in Hebrew) "across the Jordan." This would be the area known today as "the Fertile Crescent" and taking in Northern Syria eastward across the Tigris and Euphrates Valleys, not Northern Israel around the Sea of Galilee as the Gospels take it to be. This includes the "Land of Damascus" of the Damascus Document, where John the Baptist preached his ministry. This leads into the fiction of fishermen at the Sea of Galilee and the further fiction of the "brothers" Zebedee, James and John, as we described above. The prophecy of Isaiah 9:1-7, to which this passage in Matthew refers has been traditionally taken to refer to Jesus, who "withdrew into Galilee; and leaving Nazareth [he] went and dwelt in Capernaum by the Sea" when he heard that John had been arrested (Matthew 4:12). Unless one knows what "the Galilee of the Gentiles" is actually referring to, one might mistakenly assume this means the Sea of Galilee, leading to the error of placing the Isaiah prophecy on Jesus and not John where it belongs. It is Galilee "of the Gentiles" not "of the Jews" of Northern Israel. The "Nazareth" of Matthew's account will not appear in the Isaiah source. It is a corruption of "Nazoraean" or "Nazarite," as we saw above. There is scant evidence Nazareth even existed in Christ's day. It probably got into the Gospel accounts because by then it did, and Gospel writers grabbed on to the location because they needed to explain (or explain away) "Nazoraean"/"Nazarite." This same misplacement of prophecy occurs with Isaiah 40:3 and the voice "crying" in "the wilderness" to prepare "the way" of the Lord. All these key words in quotations are associated with John the Baptist and the "zeal" (v 9:7, another key "code word" for Qumrans' Ebionites) of the ascetic followers of John who "make straight a highway for our God" in "Perea" east of the Jordan. How convenient it was for Matthew to simply move John out of the way with his arrest, so that Jesus could take over the role of the prophesied "great light." The "great light" is John, *not* Jesus. Jesus told us so (John 5:35, Matthew 11:13). Other purposefully misleading polemics arise in numerous instances in the Gospels surrounding what is permissible in regards to table fellowship and manners. Both Mark 6:6-7 and Matthew 15:7-9, for example, attack those of Jamesian persuasion as "vain," a word with much significance in Qumran literature as also "lips" and "heart" in describing that which distinguishes sacred from profane, with accusations of teaching "as their doctrines the commandments of men," meaning, "traditions of the Elders" (Mark 7:5 and Matthew 15:2), not only an attack on what in Rabbinic parlance would be called "oral tradition," but an attack on James' adherence to the Torah by insisting on hand washing before eating. Likewise eating with Gentiles. The authors of these Gospels, it is now clear with the discovery of the Scrolls from Qumran, knew of these positions of the Jamesians and were intent on countering them with inventions for Jesus to espouse, thereby denigrating them. As Eisenman puts it, here you have the reason why Plato feared such persons—the poets—in his ideal Republic as a threat to the community who would spin such "mystery"-oriented "miracle tales" in order to mislead the people.

Clear evidence of the intentional writing-out of scripture of the existence of other Masters is Malachi 3:1-2. The version used in all modern Bibles is based on a 9th century standard Hebrew Masoretic text. A copy of Malachi found at Qumran among the Dead Sea Scrolls predates that by nearly ten centuries. Compare the two:

"'Behold I send my messenger to prepare the way before me, and the Lord whom you seek will suddenly come to his temple; the messenger of the covenant in whom you delight, behold, he is coming says the Lord of hosts. But who can endure the day of his coming, and who can stand when he appears? For he is like a refiner's fire and like fuller's soap.'"—RSV

"'Therefore behold I send my messenger, and he shall prepare the way before me. And *they* will suddenly come to his temple, the

Lord whom you seek and the messenger of the covenant, whom you desire; behold he himself comes, says Yahweh of hosts, but who can endure *them* when *they* come?'"—Dead Sea Scrolls

This is perhaps the prophecy that later Judaic and Essene faithful relied on for believing a two-Messiah return. Well, that isn't quite correct. The "temple" the Lord comes to is the body. "The Lord whom you seek"—in this case John—is the Master. The "messenger in whom you delight" is "the Word"—the Lord in his spirit form—because "behold *he himself* comes, but who can endure *them?*" This is unforgivable, barefaced dissembling. The intent of the writer is clear. The Lord and his "messenger" *are One*. By separating the two, Gospel writers were free to claim John was simply a forerunner of Jesus, not the Lord incarnate. That would present a problem for early church leaders in controlling the flock. One dead Messiah is easier to lay claim to than a continuing series of them. It's difficult to say when the scribal changes were made. We can, however, see why.

More research is needed, but it appears that Jesus' other two brothers, Theudas ("Jude") and Simeon bar Cleophas (Simon or Simeon "son of" Cleophas—not Joseph), both became Masters after Jesus, serving concurrently, and were themselves also martyrs. Acts 5:36-37: "For before these days Theudas arose, giving himself out to be somebody [a Master], and a number of men, about four hundred, joined him; but he was slain and all who followed him were dispersed and came to nothing [in Luke's estimation]. After him Judas the Galilean arose in the days of the census [chronology wrong], and drew away some of the people after him; he also perished, and all who followed him were scattered." This bit about

Judas the Galilean Luke lifts from Josephus' Antiquities and both dates Acts as after Antiquities' publication in 93 CE (the Census was 7 CE) and shows the source for his anachronism by confusing someone's execution following Theudas' with the notice as related by Josephus in his work of Judas the Galilean's *two sons* execution, in 48 CE which immediately follows details of Queen Helen's famine relief mission in 46 CE, with their father Judas and mention of his role in the revolt against Cyrenius four decades earlier. This "Judas the Galilean" could really be Simeon bar Cleophas, yet another written out and minimized relative of Jesus, or perhaps it really does pertain to Judas' two sons (they were paralleled as "sons of Zebedee" John and James in Matthew 20:23 as "drinking the cup" that Jesus drank). The reason we know Luke draws on this account in Josephus and the subsequent crucifixion of Judas the Galilean's two sons, "James," and "Simon," is both the parallel later in Acts 12:2 when the nebulous "James the brother of John" is executed with the sword and the description by Josephus of Judas as *"that same Judas who caused the people to revolt from the Romans at the time Cyrenius came to take a Census of their belongings."* Luke confused father with sons! As Eisenman puts it: "Since Josephus loves detailing the executions of troublesome agitators of any kind, that the beheading of 'James the brother of John'—a character never alluded to in any of Paul's works either—is missing from the Antiquities is astonishing. In our view, however, *it is not missing* [italics his]. Rather the concomitant beheading of 'Theudas' at this juncture in the Antiquities has simply been replaced in Acts by the execution of this James, 'with the sword' and it is the 'brother' aspect of the whole tangle of notices *that provides the clue to this overwrite* [italics his]."

Now, having established Acts 5:37 is not Judas "the Galilean," but probably Theudas, slain in the previous verse, who is it that is "slain after him"? With the mind-boggling juxtapositions we see going on in the Luke-Acts corpus, it is hard to say with any certainty. But given the fate of every other one of Jesus' family to have had "followers," Simeon bar Cleophas would be a good candidate. Acts says this person "drew away some of the people after him" (same v 37), and we know Simeon took over the "Jerusalem Assembly" upon the death of James and led them out into the wilderness of Judea or across the Jordan in a reverse Exodus. James identifies Simeon with the exegetical powers of "the Righteous Teacher" by the four Qumranisms "the words of the prophets," "visited," "Peoples," and "Name" in Acts 15:14-15: "Simeon has related how God first visited the Gentiles, to take out of them a people for his name. And with this the words of the prophets agree." Add to this the Scrolls Habbakkuk Pesher exegesis on Habakkuk 2:3 indicating a new "Righteous Teacher" after the demise of James in material repudiating a competing exegesis by "the Lying Spouter" in a "Delay of the Parousia" parallel and one has Simeon bar Cleophas as James' heir and successor. This also reliable dates at least this scroll as first century CE. Theudas is shown by Clement of Alexandria to have connections with the well-known gnostic Valentinus, also an Alexandrian, in the mid second-century CE, establishing a link with Ebionite/Essene mysticism. Origen (185-254), an early church father who succeeded Clement shows an awareness of Theudas as a "Messianic" individual, or part of the Messianic tradition, according to Eisenman. Why is Acts so coy on these towering figures—James, Simeon bar Cleophas, and Theudas—all apparently taking up the mantle of their fallen brother/half-brother?

The author of Jude (Judas Thomas/Theudas?), brother of James (and thus Jesus—v 1:1), makes mention himself of Paul and his friends in Jude 8: "Yet in like manner these men in their dreamings defile the flesh, reject authority, and revile the glorious ones [angels—Gal. 4:9]." And Jude 17-19: "But you must remember, beloved, the predictions of the apostles of our Lord Jesus Christ; they said to you, 'In the last times there will be scoffers [Paul—DSS CD I:14], following their own ungodly passions.' It is these who set up divisions, worldly people, devoid of the Spirit." This—*the same Paul* from Revelations 2:2—companion to Luke, author of Acts.

Once you read Eisenman's work, you realize the books of the New Testament do not sit comfortable together. Rather they contend with one another. (Del Tondo believes the four Gospels very purpose was to repudiate Paul!) The main reason we know the Teacher of Righteousness is James becomes clear from both the positive affirmation of it from the Scrolls writers, and negatively from Paul's letters and the phony 2nd or 3rd century letters of 1st and 2nd Peter. Compare the obvious tension between the letter of James with the letters of Paul over the competing doctrines of "works and faith" versus "faith alone." The Judaic 1 Maccabees 2:52: "Was not Abraham found faithful in temptation, and it was imputed to him for righteousness?" supports James 2:21—not Paul, in Romans 4:3. Psalm 106:30-31, with Phinehas staying the plague and earning righteousness, isolates Paul and divides the New Testament even further. And the seeds of anti-Semitism will be found in a shamelessly twisted portrayal of early church history in both Acts and the four Gospels to the singular benefit of Paul, deflecting responsibility for Jesus' death from the Romans and

Herodians to "the Jews." The two millenium-long Jewish Holocaust to follow that miscarriage has its genesis in this intentional rewrite of history. Again, the case is too involved to make in detail here. It took Eisenman one thousand pages in James, the Brother of Jesus. This is, however, essential reading for any Christian. The book is *a must-read* for anyone wishing to understand the history of early Christianity. His follow-up volume, The New Testament Code, came out in 2006 and adds another one thousand pages of dynamite to the debate over "Who was the historical Jesus?"

Another book from Qumran is The War Scroll, which has a direct reference to multiple saviors:

"The Final Battle the Seventh Engagement
    And in the seventh [. . .], when the great hand of God shall be lifted up against Belial and against all the forces of his dominion for an eternal slaughter [. . .] and the shout of the holy ones when they pursue Assyria. Then the sons of Japheth shall fall, never to rise again, and the Kittim shall be crushed without remnant and survivor. So the God of Israel shall raise His hand against the whole multitude of Belial. At that time the priests shall sound a signal on the six trumpets of remembrance, and all the battle formations shall be gathered to them and divide against all the camps of the Kittim So [. . .] completely destroy them. And when the sun hastens to set on that day, the Chief Priest and the priests and the Levites who are with him, and the chiefs of the battle lines and the men of the army shall bless the God of Israel there. They shall say in response: "Blessed is Your name, O God of gods, for You have done wondrous things for Your people, and have kept Your covenant for us from of old. *Many times You have opened the gates*

of salvation for us for the sake of Your covenant. And You provided for our affliction in accord with Your goodness toward us. You, O God of Righteousness, have acted for the sake of Your name."

This mention of *"gates of salvation"* is clearly in reference to *Masters,* plural. It wouldn't be possible to ascribe another logical reading here. Like most "battles" in scripture, this "seventh" (holy number of completion) and "final" battle is spiritual in nature. "Your name," as we shall see later in chapter two, has a special meaning in scripture.

Another find at Qumran, Dead Sea Scroll Fragment 4Q521, known as "A Messianic Apocalypse," begins: "[the hea]vens and the earth will listen to His Messiah, and none therein will stray from the commandments of *the holy ones."* What "holy ones" who give "commandments" could this be referring to except multiple Masters/Saviors, even if only one is specifically mentioned?

Islam shares an interesting connection to Paul's salvation "by Faith" doctrine. Like Paul pointing to Abraham's justification by faith before Moses handed down the Law (even relating in Romans 4:11-12 how his circumcision was reckoned as "a seal" of his righteousness), Muhammad follows suit by claiming *"Abraham's Religion"* came before both Judaism and Christianity, before they could "corrupt" the purity of Abraham's righteousness with *their lies* (Koran 2:145-56). Using the phrase "their lies" ties in with common "lying" themes in the Letter of James, the Dead Sea Scrolls and, especially, Paul's letters, where Paul clearly shows defensiveness at being labeled by his Jamesian opponents as "liar." Many stories of "Arabian Prophets" in the Koran—namely, Ad, Thamud, Hud, and Salih, show links to earlier sources—legendary heroes of Northern Mesopotamia Adi (Addai/Thaddeus), Thomas (probably Judas Thomas, Judas Barsabas or Jude the brother of James), and James ("Salih" is Arabic for "Righteous One"), respectively, all figures in Jamesian Judaic Christianity, centuries earlier. Muhammad acknowledges a connection with both Jews and Christians through an intermediary group, those called "'the Sabaeans'" in the Koran, all three described as "believing in Allah and the Last Day [one's death] and doing good works." "Those who believe [in the Qur'an], and those who follow the Jewish [scriptures], and the Christians and the Sabians, and who believe in Allah and the Last Day, and work righteousness shall have their reward with the Lord: on them shall be no fear, nor shall they grieve" (2:62, Abdullah Yusuf Ali translation), repeated as "do deeds of righteousness, and establish regular prayer [meditation] and charity" (2:277)—Jamesian Abrahamic salvation through *"Faith ['Belief'* in Allah] *and works* [prayer] *together.'"* In Arabic, John the Baptist is known as "as-Sabi," meaning "Baptizer," or "Immerser," showing the connection that way as well, reinforced by Hippolytus, who identifies the "Sobiai" with the "Elchasites," from the Arabic "subba," meaning "to immerse," and Epiphanius, with a similar root word, in his "Masbuthaeans." One group of these "Peoples of the Book," as Islam calls them, of whom Muhammad seems to have personal knowledge and is particularly fond, "recite the revelations of Allah *in the night season,"* strikingly similar to Josephus' description of the Qumran Ebionites, especially when Muhammad mentions their "enjoining right conduct, forbidding indecency, and vying with each other in good works, *for they are of the Righteous* ['Salihin'—'Salih,' pl.]" (3:113-4). We will revisit the theme of nighttime "reciting the revelations" of Allah in the next chapter.

Chapter Two

The Word

In chapter one the Father gave Jesus "work" to do. What "work"?

The "work" is initiation into the "Word."

Jesus, speaking to Pontius Pilate, John 18:37: "'Every one who is of the truth *hears my voice.*'" Many heard him speak, of course, but none before or after his ministry. This passage actually has a deeper significance, lost on Pilate, and most everyone else, because "voice" means his "Spirit" or "Word"—the giving out of which is "to bear witness to the truth" that is his reason for having "come into this world." The Masters bestow salvation to those for whom they so choose it. It is a *gift*, bestowed *personally*. Jesus, Mark 4:14: "'The sower sows *the word.*'" The sowing doesn't require a sacrifice. He *gives* it to those *that are given him.*

Jesus, John 14:12-13: "'Truly, truly, I say to you, he who believes in me will also do the works that I do; and greater works than these will he do, because I go to the Father [die and ascend]. Whatever you ask in my name [the Holy Spirit] I will do it, that the Father may be glorified in the Son [their Master in spirit *within them*].'" Jesus is sending his disciples out to initiate ("the works that I do") *their own* disciples. Their "works" are "greater" because he wants to deflect importance from *his* works *after he is gone*.

Jesus, John 15:16: Still speaking to his disciples in his farewell address to them, Jesus says: "'You did not choose me, but I chose you and appointed [ordained—KJV] you that you should bear fruit and that your fruit should abide; so that whatever you ask the Father in my name, he may give it to you.'" Here Jesus is showing how *he* does the choosing, not the disciple, and that they are to bear fruit, which could mean either "accomplish spiritual progress," or perhaps "bring others to God" through "my name," depending on the strength of the translated word for "appointed."

John 4:34-38: After introducing himself to the Samarian woman at the well as the Messiah she sought (with no one but her to record what he said!), Jesus uses the opportunity to tell his disciples about his "food," when the disciples return from a trip to get some food. "'My food is to do the will of him who sent me, and to accomplish his work. Do you not say, "There are four months, then comes harvest"? I tell you lift up your eyes [more on 'lift up your eyes' later], and see how the fields are already white for harvest. He who reaps receives wages, and gathers fruit for eternal life, so that sower and reaper may rejoice together. For here the saying holds true, "One sows and another reaps." I sent you to reap that for which you did not labor; others have labored, and you have entered into their labor.'" While making it clear his "food" is *the word* (Mark 4:14), he goes on to say *others* have labored, and you have "entered into their labor." What does he mean? He didn't say "I" have labored. He said "*others*" have labored. This refers to himself, and the Masters, such as John the Baptist, *before* him. John himself mentions this in John 3:27-28: "'No one can receive anything except what is given him from heaven. You yourselves bear me witness, that I said, I am not the Christ, *but I have been sent before him.*'" He isn't saying he is "heralding" him like an announcer, he is saying he was the Master *prior to Jesus*. Jesus is saying previous Masters "pass on" their spiritual power to their successors, and then, in turn, on from them *to their disciples*. This is when John goes on to say (verses 29-30) that he is the happy friend of the bridegroom (Jesus), and that he must "*decrease* [leave the scene]." Job 31:8 and Micah 6:15 cross references in the NCCC RSV for John 4:37 are not correct. The "labor" references there refer to unrewarded labor *of the disciple* when devotion to the Lord is improperly performed.

Acts 4:8-12: "Then Peter, filled with the Holy Spirit, said to them, 'Rulers of the people and elders, if we are being examined today concerning a good deed done to a cripple, by what means this man has been healed, be it known to you all, and to all the people of Israel, that by *the name* of Jesus Christ of Nazareth, whom you have crucified, whom God raised from the dead, by him this man is standing before you well. *This* is the stone which was rejected by you builders, but which has become the head of the corner. And there is salvation *in no other name under heaven given* among men by which we must be saved.'" Aside from the gratuitous slap at the Jews here (Luke's trademark), which is certainly a gloss (unauthorized addition), this speech of Peter's to the high priestly family shows that the "stone which was rejected" is "the name" of Jesus Christ—the "Word"—*not the man.* Peter was referring *to the name,* not Jesus, doing the saving: *"name OF."* The "by *him*" that allows Peter to be "standing before you well" is *"by the Word"*—*not* "by Jesus Christ"! The "name," then, by which "we must be saved and no other under heaven"—and Peter knew this applied to all time—is the "Word," *not* Jesus Christ. Interestingly, the RSV has the Greek "*This* is the stone" but the NRSV (New Revised Standard Version) has "*This Jesus* is the stone" deflecting Peter's intended understood subject—"name" of Jesus—yet another gloss!

Christians believe salvation is theirs for the asking. Paul, Romans 10:9: "Because if you confess with your lips that Jesus is Lord and believe in your heart that God raised him from the dead, you will be saved." Sorry. It does not work that way. Paul never even *met* Jesus. He is the authority? The institution of "baptism" was never meant for "all." The origin of that famous Pauline invention "'For whosoever shall call upon the name of the Lord [with "the lips," according to Paul] shall be saved'" (Rom. 10:13, KJV) is Joel 2:32, and is not about lips but about "Mt. Zion" and "Jerusalem." "And it shall come to pass, that whosoever shall call on the name of the Lord shall be delivered; for in Mount Zion and in Jerusalem shall be deliverance, as the Lord hath said, and in the remnant whom the Lord shall call" (KJV, "those whom the Lord calls"—RSV). Notice *who* is calling whom here! Clearly the Lord does the calling. The "delivered" will "call on the name of the Lord," with a mystic meaning entirely different from "calling" or "being called"—as one person would "call" another—to be covered soon, in detail. With both usages present here, this verse *proves* "calling on the name" isn't an outward "calling" like you would hail someone verbally, but an inward spiritual summoning. This is reflected in the original Hebrew Matthew (28:9): "May the name deliver you."—not the received "And behold, Jesus met them and said 'Hail!'", the standard *Greek* greeting of the day, deleted for whatever reason *(Only Jesus can deliver,* perhaps?!) from modern translations. In John 10:3 Jesus tells the Pharisees those destined for him will know him: "'To him the gatekeeper opens; the sheep hear his voice, and he calls his own sheep by name and leads them out.'" "'I am the good shepherd; I know my own and my own know me'" (v 10:14). There is no need for a Bible, no need for any book at all. Those destined for a Master will find one. Verse three has a spiritual meaning as well: the "voice" and the "name" are the "Word"—"calling" them out. In Mark 4:11-12, Jesus tells His disciples concerning "the forgiving of sins" in the "sower sowing the seed" parable: "'Unto you it is given to know the mystery [spiritual baptism] of the kingdom of God; But unto them that are without, *all these things* are done in parables, that seeing they may see, and not perceive, and hearing they may hear, and not understand; lest at any time they should be converted [initiated or spiritually baptized], and their sins should be forgiven them'" (KJV). Jesus has no intention of initiating, or "sowing the Word" in those. In the verses to follow, 13-20, Jesus explains the fruitless sowing of the Word into those who "fall away" and the fruitful sowing of the Word in those who take it to heart, "thirty-fold, sixty-fold and a hundredfold"—according to their devotion. This exchange shows both who does and doesn't *receive* initiation, and who makes the intended use of it once it *is* given.

More from the High Priestly Prayer:

Jesus, John 17:12: "'While I was with them, I kept them in thy name, which thou hast given me [this is no ordinary name here—the "Word" was given to Jesus by God] I have guarded them, and none of them *is* [present tense] lost but the son of perdition, that the scripture might be fulfilled.'"

Jesus, John 17:14: "'I have given them thy word.'"

Jesus, John 17:18: "'I have sent them into the world.'"

Where is any mention from Jesus of souls to be saved, or "not lost," *in the future*? Does any of this leave any room for future unsaved generations? Those whom God "gave" Jesus (always past tense) were all accounted for—two thousand years ago—"having accomplished the work." Jesus Christ's "work," according to *him*, was done *before* He was crucified.

Jesus, John 17:20-21: "'I do not pray for these [Jesus' disciples] only, but also for those who believe in me through *their* word that they may all be one.'" Jesus says his disciples will initiate ("through their word" means initiation) "their" *own* disciples to believe in "me"—the Holy Spirit. These are not Jesus' disciples, *but his disciples' disciples*. Understanding the meaning of the terms and phrases is crucial to understanding the meaning of the passages. When Jesus Christ speaks, there is very specific mystic meaning to his words.

Jesus, John 12:32: "'And I, if I be lifted up from the earth, will draw all men unto me.'" doesn't refer to the crucifixion, but raising one's attention within to the level of Christ. "Lifting up" is a common metaphor for spiritual achievement in mystic teachings. Also, *not* "all men" were drawn, as we now know, so Jesus wasn't foretelling his effect on other than his followers then present.

Again, Jesus, John 12:35: "'The light is with you a little longer. Walk while you have the light, lest the darkness overtake you; he who walks in darkness does not know where he goes.'" When he is gone, so is his "light." This is mystic transcendence. Christ "lifts up his eyes" many times in the Gospels. The transfiguration (Matthew 17:1-13) on the mount is a description of Christ revealing His heavenly "radiant form" to His favored disciples Peter, James, and John. The "mountain" is metaphor for "going within" in spirit—the disciples "lifting up" their eyes in verse eight to the level of Christ's inner Spirit form: "'And when they lifted up their eyes, they saw no one but Jesus only.'" This isn't Matthew telling us the disciples simply "saw" Jesus. Look at verse nine: "And as they were *coming down* the mountain, Jesus commanded them, 'Tell no one *the vision*, until the Son of man is raised from the dead [after I am gone.]'" They were all still *seeing within*, in spirit: Jesus spoke to them "as they were coming down" from the "vision" in spirit. He wanted them not to spread the word of his magnificent powers to those not worthy (nor to those in power who were plotting to kill him). Another occasion of "lifting up my eyes" is Balaam in Numbers 24: In verse two the "spirit of God" comes over him when he "lifts" his eyes, then *his eye*—singular—"is opened" (v 3—RSV). Mountains, such as in Joel 3:18: "And in that day the mountains shall drip sweet wine" and Psalm 43:3 (JB): "'Send out Your Light and Your Truth, let these be my guide, To lead me to Your holy Mountain and to the place where You live'" are used throughout the Bible (Mt. Sinai and the "burning" bush) to symbolize the inner spiritual world with the "water" or "wine" being the Spirit, and the burning "fire" (Exodus 3:2) or the shining "like the Sun" (Matthew 17:2) the fantastic refulgence to be seen there.

Matthew 13:23: "'As for what was sown on good soil, this is *he who hears the word* and understands it.'" (Remember—*not* "reads" the word—*hears* the word! And "the word" is singular—*the one word*.) See John 4:24 and John 3:8 to see what "sowing the word" means, and why it is so important: "'God is spirit, and those who worship him must worship in spirit and truth.'" "'The wind [spirit] blows where it wills, and you hear the sound of it, but you do not know whence it comes or whither it goes; so it is with every one who is born of the spirit.'" This is the "manifesting" of thy "name"—the "word" that "they have kept" in John 17:6. The "wind" in John 3:8 derives from the Greek word, *pneuma*, which means "wind" *or* "spirit." It is *the Spirit* that "blows" or "sounds" so as to be "heard"—not "the wind." The "work" of Jesus Christ is initiation into the practice of "Hearing the Sound" of the Holy Spirit. It is an apt description of what is today known as Surat Shabd Yoga—the Yoga of the Sound Current, a type of Bhakti Yoga. "Surat" means "to hear." "Shabd" is "Word," or "Spirit," "Sound Current," or "Name of the Lord." The Shabd is of a quality which causes it to be audible internally. Surat Shabd Yoga, with at least a five hundred-year continuous history, is practiced by millions of people today, in many countries. This Yoga practice, taught by Jesus to his closest disciples, is known as "The Teachings of the Saints," or "Sant Mat," in the Eastern tradition. Its central tenet is the *living* Master, and his "Word." It was brought to the world in its current form by Tulsi Sahib, Saint of Hathras, India, in the early 19th Century. Muslims call the Shabd the "Kalma" or "Ism-i-Azam," the Sikhs, "Nam," in the Vedas it is "Udgit" or "Nad." There are actually five Shabds, corresponding to the five grand divisions of the inner spirit worlds. Spiritual literature abounds with truly thousands of references to the holy "sound" of Spirit. Some may object to the usage of Indian terms to explain what it was that Jesus Christ taught a world and an age apart, but since Sant Mat is the contemporary system most closely paralleling what these Masters of Roman Palestine taught, it is appropriate that we in today's world examine it carefully and imbibe its meaning. Interestingly, the four vows considered essential for initiation by a Sant Mat Master were all present at the Qumran and Jerusalem Jamesian communities (from the Community Rule): vegetarianism, abstention from drink (and drugs), chaste living (relations within marriage), and meditation (Qumran's "*all-night vigils* in caves," also, incidentally, present in the Gospels as "watching for an hour" in Matthew 26:40, and in Islam—Muhammad's fondness for "Peoples of the Book, reciting *revelations* of Allah *in the night season*").

Ghat Ramayan, Tulsi Sahib: "The Lord who has created the universe, the regions material and spiritual, Himself resides within the human body. He is apart from Pind, And and Brahmand [physical, astral and causal planes], and yet He is close to man and is ever present within him. His knowledge [gnosis, or "Word"] can be obtained from Saints [Masters] alone, for they give the key to the soul, which enables it to go within and realize Him. Saints reveal the way of attaching the soul to Shabd and of meeting the Lord. Those who give the true teachings of Sant Mat are looked upon by most people as slanderers of holy scriptures, for they do not try to understand the truth of Sant Mat. They pay no heed to the Saints words of profound wisdom. How can such people ever get freedom from bondage in this manner? They get all the more involved in the snares of illusion." (Pt. II, pp. 63-4, 99)

This poem from Tulsi Sahib's Shabdavali is a description of the commencement of the spiritual journey within. The account starts where the soul current gets collected in the "eye center," behind and above the two eyes, where is heard the "Unstruck Music" or "Word" of God:

> "Lightning flashed in my eye, O friend,
> And brightly did shine the light of the moon.
> I got a glimpse of the Invisible within,
> And thirst and longing for the Lord were aroused.
> My ears received the boon of Unstruck Music,
> And knowledge came like the explosion of light, O
>   friend.
> Dark clouds began to scatter and the sight
> Of the Divine Mansion was revealed unto me.
> Beyond the sun, the moon and the tunnel,*
> Tulsi beheld the abode of the Lord Almighty."

(Pt. II, Holi Marfat 1, p.36)

*"Bank Nal" or twisting tunnel, between the second and third inner regions. The "sun" and "moon" are preview visions of these regions and are mentioned in Joshua 10:12-13, as Gibeon and Aijalon (chapter five, below).

"The light of the body is *the eye*."

Listening to the "Word" or "voice of God" was central to the residents of Qumran. In a Qumran Scroll fragment from Cave 4, 4Q504, are these lines (5:9-14): "You [God] remembered your covenant, for you redeemed us in the eyes of nations, and did not abandon us among all the lands to which you exiled them, to induce in their heart a return to you and a *listening to your voice*, as you had commanded your servant Moses." *"A listening"*--not just plain "listening" as to someone's "words." That's a special *kind* of listening--*meditation* on *the Word*.

And regarding the single "eye" above, or "mind's eye" of Matthew 6:22: "'The light of the body is the eye [singular]; if therefore thine eye be single, thy whole body shall be full of light'" (KJV): We have all perhaps seen the cosmetic mark on the forehead of Indian men and especially women. This is called a "tilak" and is originally representative of this spiritual all-seeing "eye" of the soul, midway between and above the eyes. In mystic literature it often appears as the place of God's "seal" or "baptism." Muslims refer to it as the "Nuqta-i-Swaida," and Hindus, the "Tisra Til." The Book of Revelation 7:3 has the angel appearing to John and "saying, 'Do not harm the earth or the sea or the trees, till we have sealed the servants of our God [disciples] upon their foreheads.'" In Matthew 7:14, Jesus says "'strait [narrow, arch.] is the gate, and narrow is the way, that leadeth unto life, and few there be that find it'" (KJV). "The gate" is the spiritual inner "eye." This "eye" of the mind and soul, incidentally, also appears on the dollar bill as the symbol of Divine Providence. The pyramid beneath the eye is representative of the human body in Egyptian lore with the Kether, or "crown," subtle energy center of the Jewish Kabbalah—The Sahasrara chakra of Eastern mystic tradition—radiating downward as through the inverted "tree of life" of the "Garden of Eden"—another representation of the body. (The Egyptians originally capped their Great Pyramid of Cheops with a capstone of pure gold, representing this all-seeing "eye of the soul," gateway to the netherworld. It must have meant a lot to them!) All the true Masters who have ever come—in all of recorded history—taught the method of opening inner sight at this "third" eye, or "single" eye. The goal for their disciples is life in the higher spheres, and ultimately union with God.

Genesis 3:5: "For God knows that when you eat of it your [inner] eyes will be opened and you will be like God, knowing good from evil." From John Daniel, Scarlet and the Beast: A History of the War between English and French Freemasonry, Vol. III we have a succinct explanation of esoteric eyesight:

"The Serpent promised Adam and Eve that their eyes would 'be opened' if they ate of the fruit of the tree of knowledge of good and evil. The key word in this passage is eyes, which in Hebrew can be translated 'knowledge.' Opened can be translated 'broadened.' What the Serpent promised Adam and Eve was that knowledge would be broadened if they ate of the forbidden fruit. But the most foreboding aspect of this scripture emerges from the fact that the Hebrew word for 'eyes' was not plural, but singular. What the Serpent actually told Adam and Eve was that their 'eye' would be broadened by knowledge. The 'eye' that Scripture wants us to consider is not the physical organ of sight, but the eye of the mind or the soul. This singular 'eye' is called the 'third eye' of clairvoyance in the Hindu religion, the eye of Osiris in Egypt, and the All-Seeing Eye in Freemasonry."

Waiting for his arrest in Gethsemane:

Jesus, Matthew 26:40: "'So, could you not watch with me one hour?'" "Watching" or as some authorities have it—"keeping awake"—applies to keeping away from "temptation" and is paired with prayer, but is also different, as is apparent in the next verse. It isn't likely that Jesus wants his disciples simply "praying" *for an hour*. Matthew has Jesus three times saying "watch." To Peter and the two sons of Zebedee, "remain here, and *watch* with me" (v 26:38), the above verse 40 to Peter, and then verse 41, also to Peter: "'Watch and pray that you may not enter into temptation; the spirit indeed is willing, but the flesh is weak.'" "Watching," or as the footnote in the RSV says "keeping awake," has something to do with avoiding temptation, and it is done "for an hour." That is meditation—sustained mental effort on a single object, or no object. In the apocryphal Gospel of Mary, Jesus teaches Mary that man is composed of soul, spirit and mind, with the mind between the soul and spirit, and that the inner "vision" of him is seen with *the mind*. "He answered and said to me, 'Blessed are you for you did not waver at the sight of me. For where the mind is, there is the treasure.' I said to him, 'How does he who sees the vision see it [through] the soul [or] through the spirit?' The Savior answered and said, 'He does not see through the soul nor through the spirit, but the mind which [is] between the two—that is [what] sees the vision'" (vv 10:10-20). It takes concentration and much practice in meditation ("watching") to still the mind. The Weymouth New Testament translation of John 6:40 has perhaps that verse's best sense of "seeing": "For this is my Father's will, that every one *who fixes his gaze on the Son of God* and believes in Him should have the Life of the Ages, and I will raise him to life on the last day." One-pointed mental concentration is instrumental in the "works righteousness" effort of "seeing" the spiritual Son *within oneself*—the real salvation of the disciple. Jesus Christ is seen, therefore, from these references to "hearing the sound" and seeing the light "fill the body" at the "single eye"—"*watching* with me"—as a teacher of the mystic path of meditation.

Many people, including some Christians, are surprised to learn that there are many "gospels"—not just the familiar Matthew, Mark, Luke, and John. If one looks carefully at the gnostic gospels of Nag Hammadi one will see many traces of these teachings as related by some of his closest disciples. It is no surprise that these gospels, having lain undisturbed for 1800 years in the desert sands of Nile Valley, show better fidelity to the original message of Christ, as they were meant for the truly chosen disciples (gnostic means "esoteric" or "secret" knowledge—"Da'at" in Isaiah 53:11), revealing secrets of initiation that orthodox clerics of the time would never have allowed to survive and "mislead" the church. No reputable scholar who has studied them doubts their authenticity, although their authorship, as is also true of many of the Bible's books, is not always known. They are historically verifiable because we have mention of some of them in other works of the time (second to third century CE) such as those of Irenaeus and Hippolytus who held antithetical views. As works reflecting the actual beliefs of early Christians, *and Christ's own disciples*, they are every bit as important as the canon. The gnostic gospel collection is so new (The Gospel of Judas was only published in 2006!), scholars are even now studying them in an attempt to place them in context. When scholars finally consider the "Rosetta Stone" of modern Sant Mat, the real mystic message of Christ will be fully explained to all, and the truth of Jesus Christ's limited ministry will be inescapable, for this is an integral part of what is taught there.

The Bible is NOT "the word of God"—the Holy Spirit is.

"Word" never *has* meant "book" or "Bible." It means "*Spirit*"! John 1:1: "In the beginning was the Word, and the Word was with God, and the Word *was* God." Jesus taught "the Word"—and the New Testament didn't appear for another two centuries! "'It is written, man shall not live by bread alone, but by every word that proceeds from the mouth of God'" (Matthew 4:4). The "word" (also, "words") as Holy Spirit is a common fixture in the Old Testament. Read Psalm 119 to see what this difference can mean. Nearly every line speaks of dwelling on the "word." "For ever, O Lord, *thy word* is firmly fixed in *the heavens*" (There is *no book* in heaven!); "I will not forget thy word"; "that I may live and observe thy word"; "I meditate upon thy promise"; "I keep the testimonies of thy mouth"; "I meditate on thy precepts"; "I will meditate on thy statutes"; "Thy law is my meditation all the day"—all refer to the "Word." So it is clear the "Word" is central to the practitioner's daily life, and often in the early morning hours: verse 55: "I remember thy name [word] in the night, O Lord"; and verse 62: "At midnight I rise to praise thee, because of thy righteous ordinances." And while we're speaking of Psalms—read this version of Psalm 23:1-3: "The Lord is my shepherd, I shall not want; he makes me lie down *in heavenly worlds* [green pastures]. He leads me beside *the waters of rest* ['still waters' of the Spirit]; he restores my *life* [soul]. He leads me *in right paths* [paths of righteousness] for his name's sake [i.e., the 'Word'!]." All these variants, except the first (mine), are footnotes in the NCCC RSV. Psalm 92 has the reader singing praises to the "name" "in the morning" and "by night"—"to the music of the lute and the harp, to the melody of the lyre." It is not likely we are to stay up at night rocking out—these are internal sounds of the Spirit we are to hear! Psalm 42:8: "By day the Lord commands his steadfast love; and at night *his song* is with me, a prayer to the God of my life." Devotees are to *meditate* on "the Word" *through the night*. And the Bible isn't the only Scripture to dwell on the "Word" or "Name." The Guru Granth Sahib, for example, holy book of the Sikh religion, abounds with hundreds, perhaps even thousands, of references to "Word" or "Nam." Sri Rag M 4., P. 79: "Through ages upon ages, through all time, through eternity, the Guru's Family increases manifold; The Family of the True Guru runs through all the Ages; by the Guru's Grace *they all Dwell upon the Name.*" Also, Surah 73: 1-5 in the Qur'an: "O you in folded garments! Stand (to prayer [meditation]) by night, but not all night, Half of it, or a little less, Or a little more; and recite the Qu'ran in slow, measured rhythmic tones. Soon shall We [Lord and 'messenger' Master] send down to you a weighty Message [the Word]."

Wonder why people are always "calling on the 'name' of the Lord" in the Bible? It's the same reason Jesus' "name that is called upon" *isn't* "Jesus." His "Name" is "the Word." "Calling on the name of the Lord" is listening to the "Word"—or Holy Spirit, or Shabd—the Spirit of God in power or action mode. In the Bible, it comes as early as Genesis, with Seth—Adam's son, born to replace the slain Abel (Gen. 4:25). Genesis 4:26: "At that time men began to call upon the name of the Lord." Seth—as perhaps the first Master in the Bible—generated a sizable following: the Sethians. Old Testament prophets often refer to the chosen as being "called by name." Amos 9:11-12: "'In that day I will raise up the booth of David that is fallen and repair its breaches, and raise up its ruins, and rebuild it as in days of old; that they may possess the remnant of Edom and all the nations who are called by my name,' says the Lord who does this." It is a calling. "Fearing the name of the Lord" is akin to not "denying" the name. In Revelation 3:8, the risen Jesus says, "I know your works. Behold I have set before you an open door, which no one is able to shut; I know that you have but little power, and yet you have kept *my word* and not denied *my name*." He means by "not denied" *not ignoring* the spiritual practice He has taught, not that He was being disavowed.

Hebrew Matthew has a different "name" in Matthew 28:19-20 from the received Greek. The "Trinity" three-part "name *OF* the Father and *OF* the Son and *OF* the Holy Spirit" is a scribal concoction, not in original Matthew at all:

Tabor blog: "Lack of Trinitarian formula for baptism in Matt. 28:19-20 is unique but seems to be in codices that Eusebius found in Caesarea: he quotes (H.E. 3.5.2): 'They went on their way to all the nations teaching their message in the power of Christ for he had said to them, "Go make disciples of all the nations *in my name* [italics mine].""

Matthew 28:19 (NIV): "'Therefore go and make disciples of all nations, baptizing them in the name of the Father and of the Son and of the Holy Spirit,'"

Original Matthew has merely *"THE NAME"*. That's "the Word", *not* "Father" or "Son", but *only* "Holy Spirit" as Word or Shabd. One of two things: Scribes either didn't know ("gnosis") the name as Word, or *did* and wanted—or were told—*to hide it* behind *the man* Jesus. This alone is proof enough to this writer that Hebrew Matthew is authentic, but when added to the John the Baptist Hebrew Matthew information that was shown to be corrupted by Tabor in chapter one, the case only becomes that much stronger. Remember—always corruption *toward* "Jesus is Lord," *never away.*

In the final chapter of Jesus' Words Only, Del Tondo asserts the need for works righteousness (or "justification") for one's salvation as shown in the exchange in Luke 19 between Jesus and Zacchaeus. If we disregard Paul's requirements (verbal confession and belief in Jesus, Romans 10) and look at "Jesus' words only," in an "actual concrete example of a person Jesus said received salvation" we find Zacchaeus giving "half of my goods" and repaying "fourfold" anyone he may have defrauded (as a tax collector). Jesus tells Zacchaeus, "'Today salvation has come to this house'" (19:9). Del Tondo rightly observes that more than faith is needed for salvation, in what takes the form here of action of repentance, but what he fails to acknowledge is the understood reality of *Jesus' presence with* Zacchaeus. The disciple must be present with his Master *physically* for salvation (John 6:40). Del Tondo asks rhetorically, "If we had Jesus' words alone, what would be the meaning of salvation promised to the thief on the cross? All the thief says is 'Jesus remember me when you come in your kingdom' (Luke 23:42). Jesus tells us the thief will be with Him that day in Paradise. Wasn't the thief saved because he 'confessed me before men,' declaring Jesus was the king—another way of saying He was Messiah? Did not Jesus say that anyone who did this, He would then 'confess him before the angels in heaven' (Luke 12:8)?" Well yes, Jesus did say that. *But he then says this*, two verses later: "'And every one who speaks a word against the Son of man will be forgiven; *but he who blasphemes against the Holy Spirit will not be forgiven.*'" Since few understand that part, most skim right over it. How does one *blaspheme* the Holy Spirit? By ignoring it! Part of works righteousness (the biggest part!) is meditation on the "Word" of the Master. The thief probably didn't get to do much meditating before dying on the cross next to Jesus, but it is always a Master's prerogative as to who is to be saved and who isn't.

"The Son" is both "the Spirit" and the man—*not* merely a person:

Now we come to perhaps the biggest of all the many misconceptions surrounding the truth of who Jesus really was. Just as we see from the limitations of language that "the Word" is not a book, "the Son" is not only a man, but a Spirit. From the gnostic Trimorphic Protennoia (37:5): "Then *the Son* who is perfect in every respect—that is, *the Word* who originated through that Voice; who proceeded from the height; who has within him the Name; who is a Light—he (the Son) revealed the everlasting things and all the unknowns were known." From the gnostic The Teachings of Silvanus (115:15): "For all dwell in God, that is, the things which have come into being through the Word *who is the Son* as the image of the Father." Clearly, gnostic conceptualizing of "the Son" included further than human form. You should be aware that John 3:16: "'For God so loved the world, that he gave *His only begotten Son* that whosoever believes in him should not perish, but have everlasting life'" is misconstrued as Jesus, the *man.* "Only begotten" is the Holy Spirit incarnate, *not* the human Master. Clearly showing this critically important truth is John 1:18: "'No man hath seen God at any time; the only begotten Son, which is in the bosom of the Father, he hath declared [H]im.'" "Him" is God, so should be capitalized, but aside from that, if John were referring to Jesus as "only begotten Son" Jesus would be personally—physically—"in the Father's bosom." Jesus is therefore referred to here as the Holy Spirit. In John 3:17, Jesus continues, "'For God sent the Son into the world, not to condemn *the world,* but that the world might be saved through him.'" Jesus isn't saying he will do it in his own person, limited as he is by time and space. *The Spirit* in His human incarnations—the Masters—will do it. He is only concerned with the souls "given" him by the Father. The only begotten Son—*the Spirit*—will see to the others. In John 3:18, "the name of the only Son of God" in "'He who believes in him is not condemned; he who does not believe is condemned already, because he has not believed in the name of the only Son of God.'" isn't Jesus, it's "the Word." The past tense in John 3:19 "'And this is the judgment, that the light has come into the world, and men *loved* darkness rather than light, because their deeds were evil'" shows, as shown earlier, that Jesus is speaking *not* about himself, but all Masters—some already departed: John the Baptist, for example. He would otherwise have said "are loving" darkness or just "love" darkness. This confirms that the famous verse 3:16, three lines before, is not *only* about Jesus, *but about all Masters who come to the world.* Upon closer examination all is not as it first seems! In the Bible,

"The Son"—therefore—can mean either "the Spirit" *or the man,* Jesus, depending on the context.

Confirming this, in another gnostic book, "the Son" is "the spark of light"—not the man, Jesus:

> "And he looked at Barbelo [the Father] with the pure light which surrounds the invisible Spirit, and (with) his spark, and she conceived from him. He begot a spark of light with a light resembling blessedness. But it does not equal his greatness. This was an only-begotten child of the Mother-Father which had come forth; it is the only offspring, the only-begotten one of the Father, the pure Light"
>
> —Apocryphon of John

Yes, *that* John—the Apostle.

John 1:8: "He was not the light, but came to bear witness to the light." John the Apostle is telling us that "John the Baptist" (remember, no Jesus yet!) was not "light". He came "*to bear witness to that light*"—*not* to Jesus, *but to the Spirit within himself*—the only begotten "Son"! See now? Be careful about assumptions that mislead. Read carefully, read widely, *and understand.*

The verb tenses in verses of John's Gospel like 6:40 and 3:16 are wrongly translated into English from Greek with sometimes profound impact. As discussed in chapter one with John 6:40, "sees" and "believes" should be "is seeing" and "continues believing." John 3:16 should read "'For God so loved the world that he gave his only begotten Son, that whoever continues believing in him should not perish but have eternal life.'" The difference is evident. With the Greek progressive "present active" tense something continuous is required of the believer. Simple present, the "aorist" tense for "pisteuo" is what is conveyed by "believes" and implies a one-time decision, not a continuing action. When translated properly, John 3:16 is about *endurance*, not salvation by faith (cf. Matthew 10:22 [KJV]: "'And ye shall be hated of all men for my name's sake: but he that endureth to the end shall be saved'"). John 6:40, "'For this is the will of my Father, that every one who is seeing the Son and continues believing in him should have eternal life; and I will raise him up at the last day'" is actually about *a daily regimen of devotion to meditation*, not a recipe for being saved. You may have noticed this is exactly the opposite of one-time good-forever Pauline salvation doctrine. Paul uses the aorist in Romans 10:9: "because if you confess with your lips that Jesus is Lord and *believe* in your heart that God raised him from the dead you will be saved." Perhaps the mistranslation in John was intentional? Everyone wants to harmonize Jesus with Paul, not vice versa. In the New International Version (NIV) this deficiency is corrected some two dozen times, but curiously, never when the verb "believes" is involved. Never once does John's original intent of Jesus' "continuous salvation" doctrine come into the English text. Much could be gained by church fathers this way: Easier to gain converts—and, dupe them into believing a departed Master can save them. *John's Gospel is not Pauline one-time salvation doctrine.* It is anti-Pauline works-oriented continuous-salvation *Jesus and Jamesian doctrine.*

Eugnostos the Blessed, another gnostic tractate, which scholars believe was a non-Christian gnostic letter which influenced the parallel, Christian, Sophia of Jesus Christ, has this concerning three differentiations of what, for gnostics, appears to be their conception of "the Trinity": "The first aeon [region], then, is that of the Immortal Man, the second is that aeon of the Son of Man, who is called First-Begetter[.]" The third is that of Son of Man, who is "Savior." The Sophia of Jesus Christ has in place of this (108) "The first aeon is that of Son of Man, who is called 'First Begetter,' who has appeared. The second aeon, is that of Man, who is called Adam, Eye of Light." That which embraces these is the aeon over which there is no kingdom, (the aeon) of the Eternal Infinite God, the self-begotten aeon of the aeons [beings] that are in it, the aeon [region] of the Immortals" These non-Christian gnostics are describing a "first-begetter" Son of Man distinct from the one who is called "Savior." The non-Christian gnostics of Eugnostos show a spiritual conception first aeon Eternal Infinite God "region," or abode of aeons [beings], separate and distinct from both second aeon "First Begetter Son of Man" region, and third aeon "Savior Son of Man" region depending on whether incarnate or not ("Savior" is incarnate third aeon). By combining the first aeon of The Sophia (the Immortal Man or "Father" aeon of Eugnostos) with the "First Begetter Son of Man," or Holy Spirit, and "Savior Son of Man," these pre-Christians reveal their understanding of "the Son" as Father, Holy Spirit, *and* "Savior," the prototypical "Trinity." The cosmogony gets very complex and is a study unto itself, but one can see that at least some pre-Christians had a well-developed concept of "only-begotten Son" as spirit, as well as a spirit-level "Son of Man."

Jesus, John 10:34: "'Is it not written in your law, "I said ye are Gods"?'" That's gnosticism. No sacrificial "Lamb of God" necessary here! "Your law" came long before Jesus Christ.

John 10:35-36: "'If he called them Gods [Psalm 82:6: "You are Gods"] to whom the word of God [Holy Spirit] *came* (and the scripture cannot be broken), do you say of him who the Father consecrated and sent into the world, "You are blaspheming," because I said "I am [the] Son of God?"'" These are disciples called to God *before* Jesus was born ("came" is past tense). How can this be? *Many* have been "Sons of God" called to the Father—both Masters *and* disciples. The first were the Elohim of Genesis 6:1-4, "sons of God" who found the "daughters of men" to be "fair," "took to wife such of them as they chose," and had children with them (verses two and four). These were "spiritual giants"—not physical "giants"—or angels, as some have supposed. Jesus said angels couldn't marry or procreate (Matthew 22:30). Further references to "sons of God" occur in both the Old (e.g., Job 1:6) and the New Testaments (e.g., Luke 20:36).

Jesus never said "I am the Son of God."

In Matthew 26:63-64, Jesus answers the high priest "'You have said so'" when asked if he was "the Christ, the Son of God." But, according to Dr. Eisenman, this could never have happened—"the question is patently absurd because neither the language of 'the Christ' or 'the Son of God' relative to the Jewish Messiah had even begun to circulate in Palestine at that time, so no one in 'the high priest's house' would even have thought to phrase the question in those terms." Dr. Eisenman also states that the phrases to follow in this verse, "and you will see the Son of man sitting at the right hand of power, and coming with the clouds of heaven" are more authentically attributable to James (from early Church sources) than Jesus—or John the Baptist. In any case, these things take place spiritually, within the devoted disciple, and aren't likely to be granted someone who just called him a "blasphemer" (26:65)!

In John 10:36: "I am [the] Son of God?" The word "the" before "Son of God" is a scribal addition, not present in the earliest and best manuscripts. Young's Literal Translation: "of him whom the Father did sanctify, and send to the world, do ye say—'Thou speakest evil, because I said, Son of God I am?'" The Spirit is "the begotten Son of God" as we saw in John's Apocryphon. Jesus is referring to himself as Spirit—not the man Jesus Christ. Orthodox scribes added the definite article "the" to strengthen the case for his supposed exclusivity.

In John 9:35, we have the blind man who can now see: "Jesus heard that they had cast him out, and having found him he said, 'Do you believe in the Son of God?'" (—some versions. Here, the RSV has "Son of man"). Then, after the man asks "And who is he, sir, that I may believe in him?" John (v 9:37) writes: "Jesus said to him, 'You have seen him, and it is he who speaks to you.'"

He says of the raising of Lazarus in John 11:4 "'it is for the glory of God, so that the Son of God may be glorified by means of it'" and is *again* referring to the Spirit, not himself, because Jesus, like any true Master, never sought glory *for himself personally*, only God. These are the only four self-described "Son of God" references of Jesus Christ in the entire Holy Bible, and they don't say Jesus said he, personally, was "the Son of God."

The Gospel of Philip—another disciple—throws light on John 11:25 ("'I *am* [present tense] the resurrection and the life; he who believes in me, though he die, yet shall he live'"). "Those who say that the Lord died first and [then] rose up are in error, for he rose up *first* and [then] died." The "resurrection" (i.e., "rising up") takes place *whenever the Master chooses*—for Master *and for disciple*. It has nothing to do with death. The Masters "rise" to the spiritual realms whenever they want—without the physical body. Another amazing revelation from the Nag Hammadi Library, is from The Letter of Peter to Philip: "Then the apostles parted from each other *into four words* in order to preach." Peter tells us that the apostles, now filled with the Holy Spirit, are going out into the world (the "four" directions?) to initiate *their own* disciples! The (Second) Apocalypse of James, with its point blank reference to multiple "sons" who "see," makes it difficult to understand how scholars could continue to overlook the most important contribution of the discovery at Nag Hammadi—multiple Saviors: "This Lord who is present [came] as a son [Jesus] who sees, and as a brother [was he sought]" (46:20), "*these two who see*" (47:20). The text is difficult to follow because of lacunae (gaps in the text) from the poor condition of Codex V, but the context shows it could very well be referring to Jesus and *James himself.*

It isn't logical (and coming from God it should be *most* logical) that God's Plan would rely on the dissemination of any book, no matter how holy. A book is subject to corruptions over time (and the Bible's corruptions are many—see below) and the ones charged to spread the message are fallible. The result is predictable and is just the situation we find today: the wrong message has been spread. Who said Jesus was the universal Savior? Not Jesus. If so, where then? He *did* show—on the contrary—that *he wasn't.* What does *he* say—not Paul (in his letters), not Billy Graham, not the Pope, not the local pastor? "For this is the will of my Father, that every one who sees the Son and believes in him should have eternal life; and I will raise him up at the last day."

Regarding church authority, does not Jesus himself say "Do not call anyone on earth 'father'" (Matthew 23:9)? So, why is the Pope called "Holy Father?" Who gave the Catholic Church Apostolic Successionary rights? Not Peter, and certainly not Jesus, in spite of calling Peter a "rock." "'And they praise the men of the propagation of falsehood [church leaders], those who will come after you. *And they will cleave to the name of a dead man, thinking that they will become pure*" (Jesus to Peter, in the Apocalypse of Peter, 74:10-15). No less than early church leader Tertullian ridiculed the idea of Bishop of Rome being "bishop of bishops." The original church was in Jerusalem under James (Acts 15). The Roman church was founded by Peter ten years later. The first pope was appointed by Paul, after Peter left Rome. At the time Paul's nominee (Linus) wasn't called the pope, he was the *bishop of Rome*. As Douglas Del Tondo says, "Thus, the validity of the the lineage of the Roman Catholic church depended crucially upon Paul. If Paul were discredited, it would discredit the Roman Catholic Church virtually from its inception."

Jesus also says in the next verse in Matthew (23:10), to his disciples, "Neither be called masters," but that means to be humble (23:12), not that they aren't Masters, or at least becoming Masters, themselves. "'You search the scriptures, because you think that *in them* you have eternal life, and it is they that bear witness *to me*; yet you refuse to come to me that you may have life'" John 5:39. Jesus is saying "The written word will not save you—I [*in person*] will."

Were it not for a chance "solar halo" on October 27th, 312, the Catholic Church itself might never have been. On that day, Constantine the Great defeated the vastly superior army of Maxentius to consolidate power over the Roman Empire in a battle waged, according to historian Eusebius, after "he saw with his own eyes in the heavens a trophy of the cross arising from the light of the sun, carrying the message, 'Conquer By This'." That night, supposedly, in a dream Christ told him to paint crosses on his men's shields to lead the way to victory. The following year, Constantine declared the Edict of Milan (neither an "edict," nor from Milan) establishing religious toleration throughout the land, and allowing Christianity to become the predominant religion of the greatest power the world had ever known. At age 40, Emperor Constantine himself professed the Faith, and the Catholic ("universal") Church thereafter became the most powerful and richest institution in the history of the world, through some of the darkest periods in man's long and troubled history: the Dark Ages, the Crusades, the Inquisition, and the conquest of the New World. The corrupt Church practices (of equally corrupt doctrine!) in the Middle Ages, such as the sale of "indulgences" (paying for forgiveness of sins), led directly to the Protestant Reformation, begun in 1517 by Martin Luther's proclamation of the "Ninety-five Theses," which strongly condemned such practices. Luther gets no free pass, however. Paul's denigration of Jews as enemies of the human race, foreigners in Judea, and killers of the Lord (1 Thess. 2:14-15) inspired Luther to profess a doctrine of harassment of the Jewish people who were by then foreigners in Germany. It was his Pauline anti-Semitism which fed directly into the Nazi's eradication policy.

The reason Jesus never tells those who aren't his to look for another Master is because they aren't *his* responsibility, but others'. What convoluted logic is not necessary to "save" those who came before his birth? They had their own Masters! Elijah, for example, who raised the dead. Pretty hard to do *if you aren't Christ*—right? Jesus, John 3:13: "'No one has ascended to heaven save he who has descended from heaven, the Son of Man.'" Elijah ascended to heaven—in a whirlwind—no less, in 2 Kings 2:11. He must be "Son of Man"—and that's according to *Jesus Christ*. Elisha, also, a disciple of Elijah, "took up the mantle" of Elijah that had "fallen from him" (2 Kings 2:13). That wasn't Elijah's coat, but his "mantle" of Mastership. Who cares about a dead guy's *coat*? That Moses was a Master is seen in Exodus 33:12-17. Verse 17: "And the Lord said to Moses, 'This very thing that you have spoken I will do [go with you and your "people"]; for you have found favor in my sight, *and I know you by name* [the Word].'" Don't believe for a minute God was telling Moses He knew his "name." He was speaking of Moses as the Holy Spirit! And John 13:20: Jesus tells Peter, who protests about having his Lord wash his feet, "'Truly, truly, I say to you, he who receives any one whom I send receives me; and he who receives me receives him who sent me'"—explaining that Jesus' successors bring salvation the same as he did. Didn't Jesus say (Matthew 4:19): "'Follow me and I will make *you* fishers of men'" not "and I will make you help *me* fish"? And what kind of "angel of God'" in Luke 2:11 isn't aware that there is to be only *one* Savior (orthodox Gospel)? "For unto you this day will be born in the city of David 'a' savior, which is

Christ the Lord"—not "*the*" Savior. A message this important should be *explicit*—don't you think?

Chapter Three

"New Age" New Testament

Christians condemn reincarnation as "New Age"—but what about Matthew 11:14? "'And if you are willing, *he is* Elijah who is to come'"—speaking of John the Baptist. Jesus himself said that. So much for "new age." Other passages with a reincarnation theme are Matthew 16:13-14, 17:10-13, Luke 9:7-8, and John 9:1-3. Reincarnation was a common belief in the Hellenized (Greek) Middle East at the time of Christ. Rebirth is the result of "karma," the natural law of cause and effect. Deeds done in life, whether good or bad, bring one back into another physical body (Jesus called it "the grave" in John 5:25, 28-29). The whole concept of suffering (or reward) is inexplicable without it. Galations 6:7: "Do not be deceived; God is not mocked, for whatever a man sows, that he will also reap." Matthew 5:26: "'truly I say to you, you will never get out till you have paid the last penny.'" Only a Master has the power to intervene. John 9:1-3: "'As he passed by, he saw a man blind from birth. And his disciples asked him, "Rabbi, who sinned, this man or his parents, that he was born blind?" Jesus answered, "It was not that this man sinned, or his parents, but that the works of God may be made manifest in him.'""" That's Jesus telling his disciples that he can alter the man's karma for the better. In Luke 13:1-3, the subject of Pontius Pilate's executing of some rebel Galileans was brought up by some of his disciples. Jesus: "And he answered them, 'Do you think that these Galileans were worse sinners than all the other Galileans, because they suffered thus? No; but unless you repent you will all likewise perish.'" He was telling them to be mindful of the law of karma. The same story is told again in the next two verses about the disaster at the tower of Siloam. God created man with a free will as a birthright. It isn't His fault if we misuse it! He never wanted a bunch of automatons. We have all lived, according to the Masters, *millions* of lives, and the previous lives set the stage for those following. The "Creator God" (Satan, in actuality) of the Old Testament and gnostic gospels exacts unforgiving accounting of our every action. And since reincarnation operates *in both directions*—advancing from a lesser developed body to a better one, as well as from a better developed one to a lesser, depending on the type life previously lived—it is best to consider this life *to be your only one*, as you can't know for sure that you will ever get another human birth again. This is what is described in the dream vision called "Jacob's ladder" in Genesis 28:11-19, "angels [souls] ascending and descending on it", to and from "heaven [inner spirit worlds]". Even "good" karmas will sometimes bring one back. In any case, only human beings have the capacity to realize the God within.

There is an interesting exchange concerning karma between Jesus and his disciples at the Last Supper. After washing his disciples' feet, there is this (John 13:10): "Jesus said to him, 'He [a Master] who has bathed does not need to wash, except for his feet [this clause omitted from some manuscripts and probably a gloss] but he [a Master] is clean all over; and you are clean, but not all of you.'" He means they are, as disciples of a Master, *becoming* free of their karmas—but not totally free yet. Christians have traditionally interpreted this reference "but not all of you" as referring to the "traitor" Judas Iscariot. But with the discovery of the Gospel of Judas we now can be fairly sure he is referring *to all of them* "in part" (their karmas) and *not* just to Judas! The whole idea of a "betrayal" in the canon is suspect because it appears as an interjection of true life action in the midst of purely mystic allegorical teaching (preceded as it is in John by the foot-washing humility lesson with the deeper karmic interpretation and followed by the commandment to "love one another"). This aside does not seem to belong. As in the Gospel of Judas, John's account was perhaps originally a consensual arrangement ("betrayal" can mean "handing over"), mistranslated and then embellished by later scribes. From The Teachings of Silvanus, we see that Judas wasn't the only "son of perdition" (John 17:12): "You know that every man who is not pleasing to God is the son of perdition. He will go down to the Abyss of the Underworld." (114:20-25). There are other problems with the account of events later that night, such as Luke's bloody sweat fiction (covered by scholars Mark A. Plunkett and Bart D. Ehrman in Ehrman's The Orthodox Corruption of Scripture as an apparent docetic repudiation), and what "men of peace" might be doing with swords to defend themselves in Gethsemane (If you're thinking Luke 22:37 and Isaiah 53:12, see discussion of "midrash" below).

For those who don't trust interpretations such as the one you have in your hands, the reference to "false Prophets leading many astray" (Matthew 24:11) isn't referring to other true Masters. It refers to the many false preachers then present in the Middle East, Paul for example, whose sole claim to authority is his own declaration of a "vision" on the road to Damascus, which appears to be a redivivus of Balaam's vision in Numbers 22 and ties him securely to the condemnation of Jesus in Revelation 2:2 and 2:14 with a revisit of Balaam's permission to eat "things sacrificed idols." Matthew 24:4-5: "'Take head that no one leads you astray. For many will come in my name, saying "I am the Christ," and they will lead many astray.'" Jesus was more right here than perhaps even he could know. The correct translation, present in some more literal versions (but still with the comma after "saying") is without the quotation marks: "'For many will come in my name, saying I am the Christ, and they will lead many astray'" which alters the meaning completely when the phrase "I am the Christ"—serving an orthodox reading (more in chapter four)—ceases to be an interjection and becomes the warning Jesus intended: He isn't referring to others calling *themselves* Christ, but to them calling *HIM* Christ—*after he is gone!* This is exactly what happened leading up to the destruction of Jerusalem (Paul!) and from then on (preachers innumerable), up until the very present. Also, the admonition at the very end of the Bible, Revelation 22:18, not to "add to" or "take away" from the "words of this book" is directed at scribes who had to hand copy the manuscripts before there was mechanical printing. It isn't a condemnation of interpreters as some would have us think. John 10:7-10: "So Jesus again said to them, 'Truly, truly, I say to you, I am the door of the sheep. All who came before me [all who? he's talking about the inner manifestations of *previous* Masters and prophets who may appear as the Negative Power in disguise to a disciple, *within* himself as a vision, in an attempt to deceive him and lead him astray] are thieves and robbers; but the sheep did not heed them [they are told at the time of initiation how to test the validity of the vision]. I am the door; if any one enters by me, he will be saved and will go in and out [of the single eye] and find pasture [in the Spirit world]. The thief [false vision] comes only to steal and kill and destroy; I came [past tense—not present continuous 'am come' if Jesus was universal Savior] that they may have life, and have it abundantly.'"

The Bible's New Testament was cobbled together by early church leader Marcion (books of Luke and letters of Paul minus the vengeful Old Testament God references), bishops Irenaeus, Eusebius and Athanasius (under the protection of Emperor Constantine), and Augustine of Hippo (adding only Jude to Athanasius' list to complete the modern New Testament), in the second and fourth centuries, mostly for their own purposes. Don't be overly taken with it. Do you know why Irenaeus chose *only four* "Gospels" for inclusion in "the Bible"? It wasn't for the enlightenment of mankind:

> "But it is not possible that the Gospels can be either more or fewer in number than they are. For since there are four zones of the world in which we live, and four principal winds, while the church has been scattered throughout the world, and since the 'pillar and ground' of the church is the Gospel and the spirit of life, it is fitting that she should have four pillars, breathing incorruption on every side, and vivifying human afresh. From this fact, it is evident that the Logos, the fashioner

demiourgos [divine entity] of all, he that sits on the cherubim and holds all things together, when he was manifested to humanity, gave us the gospel under four forms but bound together by one spirit."

Against Heresies 3.11.8

Irenaeus chose the four canonical Gospels, but banned the gnostic Gospels of Mary, Thomas, Philip and John (the "Heresies"). John gets his Gospel, but *not* his Apocryphon? Why isn't the Gospel of Mary Magdalene included? The Gospel of Judas, recently published in book form and a televised special by the National Geographic Society, has this beautiful exchange between Jesus and Judas (gaps in text deleted): "Come that I may teach you about the things that no human will ever see. For there exists a great and boundless aeon [region], whose extent no angel could see, in which is the great invisible Spirit, which no eye of an angel has ever seen, no thought of the heart has comprehended, *and it was never called by any name.*" The complex cosmologies of the gnostic gospels are explored in detail in Sant Mat. The three highest realms known to Sant Mat are Alakh (the Invisible), Agam (the Inaccessible), and *Anami (the Nameless).* Does that not look like a match? These are in turn incorporated in the highest of five "heavens" or spiritual regions, that highest region being "Sach Khand" or "Sat Desh"—the eternal abode of God. Even Paul acknowledged at least *three* heavens (2 Cor. 12:2) in a heavenly experience of "a man"—probably James. They are the "many mansions in my Father's house" that Jesus speaks of "preparing for you" in John 14:2 (KJV). These regions are, we are told, real places—in Spirit—and they are vast beyond comprehension! It is said that this physical region we call "the Universe" ("Pinda") is comparable to "a basket hanging in a tree" in the next higher one above ("Anda"), and so forth, on up. Lifespans in the regions below Sach Khand are great compared to those here, but not unlimited. Many details of these regions are discussed in the gnostic collection as well as the classics of Eastern Mystic Philosophy, including some of the great spiritual poetry. Among the gnostic gospels, for example, The Apocryphon of John speaks of these five aeons, and their corresponding sounds or "shabds." "And I raised him up and sealed him in the Light of the Water [Spirit] with five seals, in order that death might not have power over him from this time on"; and the gnostic Trimorphic Protennoia has the Master promising not to leave this world "until I have revealed myself [to all my brethren] and until I have gathered together all my brethren within my [eternal kingdom]. And I proclaim to them the [five] ineffable [Seals, in order that I might] dwell in them and they also might dwell in me." This important number five will surface again later in the story of David and Goliath.

All Masters have been vegetarians. All Masters have abstained from drinking. Although there is no evidence in the Bible to establish that Jesus was vegetarian, it is possible, even probable, *that there was* and it was excised early on in the development of the canon in the quest for converts to the early church, or to expunge evidence of ascetic tendencies. Epiphanius, in Panarion 30.16.5, has the Ebionite Jesus saying: "'I came to abolish sacrifices, and unless you cease sacrificing, my anger will not cease from you.'" In Jesus' Palestine, a major source of the Temple priests' income was selling sacrificial animals to visitors. The reason Jesus threw the moneychangers out of the Temple was likely not only because he didn't approve of them making it a bazaar *but that he also didn't approve of the killing of the animals.* There *is* evidence among allied source materials of the time for showing that many, if not all, the early gnostic groups were vegetarian and not given to strong drink, as there is evidence that John the Baptist, Jesus Christ's predecessor, and many, if not all, of Jesus' principal disciples were as well. The Dead Sea Scrolls are clear about the vegetarianism and abstention of Qumran and Jerusalem Jamesian faithful. The reason they had a "camp" in the desert is because they were following the "Rechabite" tradition of Jeremiah 35:8: "We have obeyed the voice of Rechab, our father, in all that he commanded us, to drink no wine all our days, ourselves, our wives, our sons or our daughters, and not to build houses to dwell in." They were abstainers for sure—it is abundantly repeated (vv 6,7,8,14).

The famous diet of locusts and honey that John the Baptist is said to have eaten (Matthew 3:4, Mark 1:6) is doubtful. Epiphanius, in Gospel of the Ebionites, has John eating "wild honey, the taste of which was that of manna, as a cake dipped in oil" (Ex. 16:31) probably a reference to the proverbial "manna" of the ancient Israelites which is a spiritual food, not even a physical one. The Greek words for "cake" and "locusts" differ by only one letter, so it is conceivable that someone (a scribe) made a slip. In any case, who can imagine someone living on bugs? Josephus, in the Slavonic edition of the Jewish War has John saying: "'I am a man called by the Spirit of God, and I live on stems, roots, and fruit.'" And, elsewhere, "He [John] was a strange creature, not like a man at all. He lived like a disembodied spirit. He never touched bread. Wine and other strong drink he would not allow to be brought anywhere near him, and animal food he absolutely refused—fruit was all he needed." Although the author of the edition is uncertain, that the content is what it is supports John's vegetarianism. Peter is said by Clement in the Clementine Recognitions to have been vegetarian: "'I live on bread alone, with olives, and seldom even with pot herbs [vegetables].'" James, Jesus' own brother, was a vegetarian and teetotal: "He was holy from his mother's womb; and he drank no wine nor strong drink, nor did he eat flesh."—Hegesippus, in History of the Church, by Eusebius. Thomas was, as well—in the Acts of Thomas: "he fasts continually and prays [meditates], and eats only bread, with salt." And John the Apostle, in the History of John: "His sustenance was, from the ninth to the ninth hour once, when he had finished his prayers [meditating], bread and herbs with a mess of lentils, which he bought for himself [Masters are always self-sustaining—they live off no one else] as he went from town to town, eating, and drinking water only." We can be fairly sure anyone who teaches karma and resulting rebirth will be found to avoid meat eating—today, or two thousand years ago—and teaching it. Paul's New Testament rebuttals of Jamesian dietary restrictions (James 2:11,13: "For he who said, 'Do not commit adultery,' also said, 'Do not kill.' If you do not commit adultery but do kill, you have become a transgressor of the law." and "For judgment is without mercy to one who has shown no mercy; yet mercy triumphs over judgment.") about eating "whatever is sold in the market" (1 Cor. 10:25, etc.) is good evidence this was a major point of contention.

Incidentally, the idea of Jesus eating fish in His third and final resurrection appearance to his disciples in John 21 to "prove" he was not a ghost? It never happened. Because of stylistic dissimilarities and its awkward placement after two sign-off final verses in John 20, it is believed that this entire account is a gloss and not original to this Gospel at all! This is the only time John ever speaks of the disciples as being fishermen at all, and is perhaps meant to harmonize his "fishermanless" Gospel with the other Gospel accounts of "fisherman disciples." Or, it could be a ploy by dissident sects of the time to portray Jesus as a flesh and blood human (anti-Docetism), or even as a meat eater, which he most certainly *wasn't*, in a time of intense internal struggles among believers over correct doctrine (note, again, the many compromising references on meat eating and wine drinking in Paul's letters to the Romans and Corinthians, trying to defuse a hot debate topic). The fisherman stories could have grown from the fact of Jesus calling them "fishers of men"—a common metaphor for how Masters gather disciples—used in Mandaean (followers of John the Baptist; and the oldest surviving gnostic group, from present day Iraq) and Manichaean (another gnostic sect) texts—groups with which Jesus certainly would have been familiar. (They could also refer to Jesus being the herald of the Age of Pisces, the fish—see below.) The disciples became, therefore, fishermen! It would basically be Mark's word (Mark 1:16) versus John's. Andrew and Simon Peter decided to leave John the Baptist and "followed Jesus" in John 1:37, but only in John 1:43 was it that "Jesus decided to go to Galilee"—where he picked out Philip and Nathanael, not Simon Peter and Andrew.

The "world to come" at the "end of days" (death) is *an inner world* of "Spirit" and much of Matthew's colorful descriptions of the "last days" are visions of what takes place in Spirit, such as when a disciple passes on. These fantastic visions are *spirit worlds*—ones that can be seen *even while still living* (Mark 9:1-10). "God's Temple" is *in heaven* (Rev. 11:19). It is for those "who fear thy name" (v 18)—those who devote themselves to hearing "the Word." Luke 17:20-21 (KJV): "Now when he was asked by the Pharisees when the kingdom of God would come, he answered them and said, 'The kingdom of God does not come with observation ["*signs* to be observed"—RSV]; nor will they say, "See here!" or "See there!" For indeed, the kingdom of God *is within* [Gr. "entos" or *within—not* "in the midst of" (RSV)] you.'" His coming is not "here"—but "there"—in Spirit! Jesus, John 18:36: "'My kingship is not of this world.'" Why should he come *here* when "his kingdom" is *there?* Jesus is waiting *there.* He could raise any one of his own "on the last day"—death. *And he did.* They are already "in the kingdom." "'Truly I say to you, *this generation* will not pass away till all these things take place'" (Matthew 24:34). If Jesus didn't "come" then, what makes one think he is "coming" today? He *himself* said he would—so it must be some other kind of "coming," right?

Consider how Jesus himself limited his personal influence. Jesus, Matthew 28:20: "'Teaching them to observe all things whatsoever I have commanded you: and, lo, I am with you always, even unto the end of the world. Amen.'" (KJV). This is a mistranslation. The RSV has it correctly: "'Teaching them to observe all that I have commanded you; and lo, I am with you always, *to the close of the age.*'" The "age" Jesus is talking about is the "astrological age," or "aeon" of Pisces (the "fish" bumper sticker), which "closes" with the commencement of the Age of Aquarius around 2150 CE. This age is reflected in Luke 22:10: "'Behold, when you have entered the city, a man carrying a jar of water will meet you; follow him into the house which he enters.'" The sign of the constellation (and Age) of Aquarius is none other than a man pouring out a jar of water. We are to follow him into "the house" (the New Age) with our eyes open. We will find again and again how Jesus taught deep truths with storytelling.

Since, as far as can be ascertained, all the writers of the New Testament books were Jews, except the Greek Luke (if indeed he wrote Luke and Acts), one must bear in mind the lens through which came the information we have about Jesus Christ. The best example would be the virgin birth. Preceded by Horus (Egyptian), Krishna (Hindu), Dionysus and Attis (Greek), and Mithra (Persian), being born of a virgin is nothing new. The scribes who added the virgin birth story to the original Hebrew Matthew, where it is absent, were guilty of embellishing (Matthew 1:23) the Hebrew "almah" of Isaiah 7:14, meaning "young woman" (RSV), to come up with the tale of the "virgin" mother of the "Son of God." (In any case, two verses later, 7:16, "Immanuel" is given an 8th Century BCE provenance.) Dr. Eisenman contends that the virgin birth is really about *James*, as a lifelong, chaste Nazarite, whose virginity was grafted onto Mary as needed by Gospel writers to isolate Jesus from others who might be threats to Jesus' unique standing as lone "Savior." Themes such as virgin birth, three kings, heralding star in the east, slaughter of the innocents, twelve disciples, water to wine, crucifixion, three days dead (which is, of course, not the day and a half we have between Good Friday at dusk and Easter morn!), resurrection and ascension, afterlife, final judgment, circumcision, ark of the covenant, Passover, Holy Communion, Easter, Christmas, Great Flood, "Lamb of

God," etc., are all recycled themes from *other*, earlier, religious traditions (all examples are Egyptian). The Sumerian Creation Story, complete with a garden, a snake and a forbidden fruit is another example. The language-challenged builders of the Tower of Babel is another story with Mesopotamian origins. In many ancient societies, the time of the winter solstice was a major event, signaling a turning of seasons and a return of the life-giving sun, after three days "dead" at its low-point in the southern sky. The story of the magi in Matthew, bringing news of the birth of Jesus has origins as the "three kings" or stars of Orion's Belt in the constellation Orion which align every December twenty-fourth with the brightest star of the winter sky, Sirius—"the Star of the East" (Matthew 2:2)—to point at the location on the horizon where—at the spot where the "Southern 'Cross'" appears around Christmas—the sun ("Son") will "rise" on the twenty-fifth to renew all things. The Eastern orthodox symbol for Christ, the cross with the circle, is a representation of the zodiac—not a crucifixion—surrounded by the twelve astrological signs (disciples) who "travel" around with "the Son." More astrology: the sign of the virgin—Virgo—is a sheaf of wheat, yielding the fictitious birthplace, Bethlehem,which means "house of wheat" of the virgin-born savior. None other than Justin Martyr (100-165 CE), celebrated early Christian church father, said, "When we say that he, Jesus Christ, our teacher, was produced without sexual union, was crucified, and died, and rose again, and ascended into heaven *we propound nothing different* from what you believe regarding the sons of [the Roman god] Jupiter." Even Satan is borrowed. He is red for Set, the Egyptian opponent of the god Horus; carries the three-pronged fork of the Greek god Poseidon; and the horns of Pan, Greek god of forests, pastures, and flocks of *goats* (hence, the horns). There are too many threads of this theme to go into here, and they are well covered by Bishop Spong and others. What should be acknowledged by all is that writers of old were writing in the style of the times for the people of the times in which they were writing. The utter and complete confusion today over the true message of God's plan for mankind, even mankind's very makeup (Consider: "Made in his image" does not mean made to "look" like Him. It means made to reflect His spiritual constitution in the finer planes of creation—ones we have descended through in our devolution into the physical body and through which we may return to Him) shows how mistaken we can be when relying on ancient sources for our information.

The "rapture"—a grand reunion of all believers "in the clouds, in the air"—of 1 Thessalonians 4:13-18, is hugely misread. "For we would not have you ignorant, brethren, concerning those who are asleep [dead], that you may not grieve as others do who have no hope. For since we believe that Jesus died and rose again, even so, through Jesus, God will bring with him those who have fallen asleep. For this we declare to you by the word of the Lord, that we who are alive, who are left until the coming of the Lord, shall not precede those who have fallen asleep. For the Lord himself will descend from heaven with a cry of command, with the archangel's call, and with the sound of the trumpet of God. And the dead in Christ shall rise first; then we who are alive, who are left, shall be caught up together with them in the clouds to meet the Lord in the air; and so we shall always be with the Lord. Therefore comfort one another with these words." Ok, we all agree the "fallen asleep" are the dead. The "word of the Lord" is, again, the "Word" or Spirit. Those left alive "until the coming of the Lord" are those believers who will see their Master—*within themselves!*—in spirit form, *while living.* That's why the dead "precede" the living: *they are already with the Lord.* The "cry of command," "the archangel's call," and the "trumpet" all signify the sharp jolt of the sudden appearance of *the inner Master* (his "astral" form) inside the believer (*not* the whole world) and his resounding attendant "Word" or "Shabd." The dead in Christ "will rise first"—they went up when they died—and then those "who are left" shall be caught up together with them "in the clouds" (of *heaven*—not our sky) to meet the Lord "in the air" (i.e., in the Spirit).

Chapter Four

The "Inerrant," "Original" Bible

The writers and scribes of the Bible made mistakes. For example, Matthew (27:9) sets the price on Jesus' head at "thirty pieces of silver" and then attributes the amount to Jeremiah's prophecy, when it really was Zechariah's (11:12-13). This was a scribal error when transcribed from the Hebrew Matthew to the Greek. More to the point, and much more egregious is Paul being misled about what the Lord said to Abraham by an erroneous translation in the Septuagint (247 BCE) of the Hebrew of Genesis 15:6. "And he [Abraham] believed the Lord; and he reckoned it unto him as righteousness. According to Douglas Del Tondo in Jesus' Words Only, Abraham, not God, is clearly the actor reckoning something as righteous: "Paul interpreted the verse to mean God imputed righteousness to Abraham based on faith. From this [and Habakkuk 2:4] Paul deduced salvation based on Abraham's faith alone (Gal. 3:6-9; Rom. 4:3)." Paul is therefore claiming Genesis 15:6 is about Justification by Faith, his pet doctrine. We know from chapter one that is contrary to James' teachings which in his letter are abundantly clear on works righteousness, and also Jesus' teachings (Matthew 25:31-46). Habakkuk 2:4: "the righteous shall live by his faith" is also a mistranslation. "Faith," "pistis" in Greek is wrong. It should be "faithfulness"—"emunah" in Hebrew. Just as in chapter one with "He" being not Abraham but God, again Paul used the faulty Greek Septuagint. "Faithfulness" connotes continuous action, not one-time belief. Del Tondo investigates in exhaustive detail how Paul got it wrong on faith vs. works righteousness. Like so much in this field, trouble lurks in the translation. But, *not only* in translation. Without exposure to mystic teachings the deeper significance of many passages is lost. Del Tondo uses Deuteronomy 9:23: "And when the Lord sent you up from Kadesh-barnea, saying, 'Go up and take possession of the land which I have given you,' then you rebelled against the commandment of the Lord your God, and did not believe him *or obey his voice*" to show how faith and obedience go hand-in-hand, unlike for for Paul with stand-alone faith salvation, without recognizing the primary import of the passage with emphasis on "obeying" his voice—the "*Word.*" The "works righteousness" brought by all Masters is the path of spiritual meditation—listening attentively to *his Holy Name.*

A written document is subject to many forms of corruption, additions, and losses. Before we get into the corruptions and additions we should look at a clear indication of what has been lost. Douglas Del Tondo relates the obvious case of 1 Chronicles 29:29: "Now the acts of King David, from first to last, are written in the Chronicles of Samuel the seer, and in the Chronicles of Nathan the prophet, and in the Chronicles of Gad the seer, [with accounts of all his rule and his might and of the circumstances that came upon him and upon Israel, and upon all the kingdoms of the countries (29:30)]." They're gone. The Chronicles of Samuel, Nathan and Gad are forever lost to us. Who knows what might have been written within them? Maybe someone was offended or threatened by what they contained. We will never know. What we do know is that according to 1 Chronicles they were all inspired writings. 1 Samuel 9:9 says a "seer" was a prophet. What kind of God would let this happen? Maybe written scripture isn't what it's cracked up to be. The Bible for thousands of years has limped along with at least three of its witnesses missing. Another might be the Shepherd of Hermas, a very popular work among early Christians, dropped from the canon in 397 CE. Still another would be the Book of Enoch, Enoch being mentioned in Jude 14, by none other than the brother of the Lord Jesus (Judas Thomas/Theudas/Thaddeus) and most likely not just a prophet, but a true Master like John, Jesus and James. This book has been part of the canon of the Ethiopian Christian Orthodox Church for two thousand years and was part of the universal canon until 363 CE when the Roman Catholic Church dropped it at the Council of Laodicea without explanation. Like Trent and Nicea, this "Council" decided what would be read by the rest of the faithful with no accounting of why the ones voting should have had that authority (kind of like Paul's). This is most striking when one considers books that *did* make it, like blatantly forged Second Peter (3:15, about Paul, could never have been written by Peter)—almost universally recognized as undeserving of inclusion in the canon. Martin Luther in 1522 rejected the books of James and Revelation because they contradicted Pauline doctrine. They are two of the only three (with Jude) that can be considered authentic of the whole twenty-seven. Fortunately they have been retained, because from these three alone we can deduce the counterfeit Pauline influence present in the others, without even resorting to the Dead Sea Scrolls or Nag Hammadi books. These three are the only books in the New Testament written or inspired by true Masters.

While Donald Morgan's Website listing hundreds of Bible inconsistencies (not necessarily "contradictions") may not be a Christian's favorite online site, it does serve to point out the fact that proving "inerrancy" would be problematic at best. Scribal changes—both accidental and intentional—to the biblical manuscripts, all handcopied many times over from antiquity, have made the modern Bible an unreliable guide for unquestioned Truth as Christian organizations of today would have us believe. The idea of an inerrant biblical "Word of God" is relatively recent, which is in itself curious, since we now have more evidence than ever of variations from the original texts. Biblical scholars have documented many of these changes—so numerous that some estimate that there are more variants in the manuscripts than there are words in the texts! Flat-out forged additions include the woman caught in adultery (John 8:3-11), the ending of Mark (vv 16:9-19), the entire concluding chapter of John, the Trinity (1 John 5:7), Luke's "blood of the new covenant" (vv 22:19b-20), and the "bloody sweat" (Luke 22:43-44). Some additions and changes create corruptions in vitally important concepts such as "the Son" as "Spirit" in "I am ['the', scribal addition] Son of God" of John 10:36, and the advent of other Masters besides Jesus in John 9:4: "'We must work the works of him who sent me [should read "*us*"], while it is day; night comes, when no one can work.'" The disagreements between Gospel accounts are well documented. In John Shelby Spong's excellent Resurrection: Myth or Reality?, the diverse scenarios of the "empty tomb" story—four Gospels, four versions—are well covered. It is beyond the scope of this treatise to cover it adequately here. Check out a Gospel Parallel Bible (e.g., "The Five Gospels Parallels" website) for a look at this amazing work of story fabrication. Also see Dr. Bart Ehrman's The Orthodox Corruption of Scripture which covers well some of the intentional changes to Scripture (primarily attempts by scribes to counter docetic and adoptionistic apologists).

All can turn on a single word. We saw in chapter one how even a single *letter* sometimes makes all the difference, as with "he [He, KJV] reckoned" (Gen. 15:6). Never forget that all the information we have on Jesus comes from second, and sometimes third, translations, from the oral original. Much of the meaning of the original message depends on the translation. If mistranslated (usually from the Greek) by mistake or ignorance, the real meaning of a sentence can be lost. Already mentioned is the critical mistranslating of the present active tense Greek verbs in the original manuscripts of John's Gospel, yielding *opposite* simple present English readings instead of the more correct English continuous present. Here's the list for "is believing", not "believes": John 1:12; 3:15, 16, 18, 36; 5:24; 6:35, 40 (with "is seeing"), 47; 7:38; 11:25-26; 12:11, 37, 44, 46; 14:12; and 17:20. The point, as Del Tondo *partially* perceives, is that the theme of John is that one must "endure" in belief for salvation to be realized, not that a one-time faith saves--but beyond that—that one must *continue* "seeing" the Master (in meditation) in order to resurrect (John 6:40). A classic example of mistranslation is 1 Timothy 6:10a. Newer Bible versions have the correct "For the love of money is 'a' root of all evil."—not "the" root of all evil.

It makes quite a difference in meaning. We see this with Jesus in Matthew 6:22 when translators of the Revised Standard Version tried to "update" or "fix" the King James without knowing what they were doing. There are other references to "the single eye" or "eye center" (Num. 24:3, for example), so we know that the eye in Matthew 6:22 is "single"—as in the KJV—and not "sound"—as in the RSV. This is an example of a translational choice by the translator. Usually, the RSV has the more correct translation, but in this case, somebody just wasn't familiar with the way one's body "fills with light"! In the apochryphal literature there is a clear example of this in The Teachings of Silvanus, from the Nag Hammadi Library, where the Greek noun "logismos" corresponding to the modern "dialogismos" (literal meaning "by means of Logos" or "Word") is rendered "reasoning power" ("Before you can drink of it [the true wine, or 'Word'], you must cultivate your 'reasoning powers.'") while the correct sense of the word is "meditation" as is clear from where it is used elsewhere with contextual support, such as Socrates in Plato's Phaedo: "She [the soul] will calm passion by listening [by 'logisomos'] to the Logos within." It's not likely that "reasoning power" will "still passion." The correct translation would be "meditation" on the Logos, not "reasoning" on it. This simply betrays the natural bias of scholars to the rational explanation rather than the esoteric or mystical one, which is, in spiritual literature, the correct one. It is a problem that comes up not just in translations, but is common in exegeses of both canon and apocrypha.

Fortunately, good work is being done presently in rectifying the misperception that the Bible is without flaw. In his comment section of Misquoting Jesus, Dr. Ehrman states "But truth be told, I have not been surprised by the interest the book has generated. After all the book gives interesting—and largely unknown—information about what lies behind the Bible, which is the most widely read, revered, studied, proclaimed, (and, arguably, misunderstood) book in the history of Western Civilization. Most people had no idea that we don't have the original copies of any of the books of the New Testament, that the copies we do have are for the most part centuries removed from the originals, and that all of those copies have mistakes in them, making it difficult in some places to know what the New Testament writers actually said. In some places we may never know. But this is information that readers of the New Testament have a right to know! It should not simply be tucked away in footnotes, but should be loudly proclaimed in Christian education classes, by Christian leaders and educators, in books about the Bible, and in editions of the Bible. This is information that is crucial for our understanding of the Bible, the most important book—whether looked at religiously or culturally—in the history of our form of civilization."

Dr. Ehrman's The Orthodox Corruption of Scripture makes a substantial contribution to understanding how orthodox bias has infiltrated the scripture of the New Testament. For example, Ehrman relates the debate among orthodox scribes early in the formation of the canon concerning the wording of Matthew 24:36: "'But of that day and hour no one knows, not even the angels in heaven, *nor the Son*, but the Father only'" regarding Jesus' "second coming." The Revised Standard Version and other newer translations have the phrase "nor the Son," the King James does not. The reason scribes found the phrase problematic was that the phrase could be used by adoptionists to argue that Jesus was human, and not completely divine, because he didn't know when his Second Coming would be. The trouble the scribes had with it is evident with particular clarity in Codex Sinaiticus, an early manuscript type, where the original has the phrase, it was erased, and again written in by yet another scribe. That the phrase *could* be referring to either Jesus *or* the Holy Spirit, as has been discussed earlier, is not the point—although a debate on it would be interesting—what is important is that scribes were clearly taking liberties to alter the texts. Another alteration he weighs in on is John 1:18 in John's prologue: "No man hath seen God at any time, the only begotten Son, which is in the bosom of the Father he hath declared him" (KJV). Ehrman says "The variant reading of the Alexandrian [codex] tradition, which substitutes 'God' for 'Son,' represents an orthodox corruption of the text in which the complete deity of Christ is affirmed [like Matthew 24:36 without 'nor the Son']." Here, again, as stated before, confusion reigns in the minds of the scribes because they don't know that the Son *is* God (Word)—not because he is Jesus, but because he is *Spirit!*

"The death of Jesus in Luke-Acts is not a death that effects an atoning sacrifice. It is the death of a righteous martyr who has suffered from miscarried justice, whose innocence is vindicated by God at the resurrection" states Dr. Ehrman about Luke's Gospel. Luke departs from Mark in that the tearing of the temple curtain *occurs before Jesus' death* (Luke 23:45), just before he says, "Father into thy hands I commit my spirit!"—*not after* as in Mark. Combined with the darkness over the land, it appears to be an omen. Luke also changes the centurion's observation about Jesus' identity as God in Mark into a statement of his innocence, in keeping with his narrative's theme of Jesus' unjust persecution and death: "'Certainly this man was innocent!'" (Luke 23:47).

What is more significant in Luke, however, is the interjection of something Luke evidently *didn't even write,* which are the verses 22:19b-20. The New Testament manuscripts present Luke 22: 19-21 in six different forms of text, four of which lack internal support (word usage, etc.) and authenticity according to Ehrman. Of the two remaining texts, the shorter reads: "And taking bread, giving thanks, he broke it and gave it to them, saying 'This is my body. But behold, the hand of the one who betrays me is with me on the table'" (vv 19a, 21). The longer version includes verses 19b-20: "[And taking bread, giving thanks, he broke it and gave it to them, saying 'This is my body] *that is given for you. Do this in my remembrance.' And the cup likewise after supper, saying, 'This cup is the new covenant in my blood that is poured out for you.* [But behold the hand of the one who betrays me is with me on the table.]'" Ehrman discusses at length the debate between scholars Wescott and Hort and other commentators over which version is correct—Wescott and Hort's famous so-called "Western non-interpolation" shorter version or the better attested longer version. Ehrman argues in favor of Wescott and Hort's shorter Western version over the uncharacteristically longer Alexandrian variant in part because of the better internal support for it and partly exactly because of its against-the-grain tendency of being short. Vocabulary, style, and theology all indicate "intrinsic" probability of this being an addition not original to Luke. The phrase "for you" occurs twice in the passage in question and nowhere else in all of Luke-Acts. The Greek word for "remembrance" occurs only here, as does the item "new covenant"—and certainly nowhere else as the new covenant "of my blood." As Ehrman points out, these vocabulary inconsistencies appear not only in contrast to the rest of Luke, but in the book of Acts also. The concept is suspect as well. Nowhere else in his Gospel or in the book of Acts does Luke portray

Jesus' death as atonement for sins. Even more to the point, there is evidence Luke went out of his way *to eliminate* such a theology from what he borrowed from Mark's account. So here is persuasive evidence that a fundamental principle of orthodox Christian doctrine is a forgery—at least in Luke's contributions to the New Testament. If blood atonement was so central to the gospel's message, why is it so sparsely attested there? It only originally existed (as best as can be determined) in two of the four gospels, one of which (Greek Matthew) was borrowed.

The "bloody sweat," later in the same chapter of Luke (vv. 43-44), is revealed as an anti-docetic (Jesus suffered as a human) structural interjection: The literary device used by Luke, called a chiasmus, is a structure of several verses, 40-41 going in, 42 the focus of the chiasmus ("not my will, but thine, be done"), and 45-46 going out in reverse of 40-41, illustrating the importance of prayer in the overcoming of temptation, which is ruined by the interjection of forged verses 43-44 about the agony Jesus endures as he awaits his execution:

(a) And when he came to the place he said to them, "Pray [meditate] that you may not enter into temptation."

  (b) And he withdrew from them, about a stone's throw,

    (c) and knelt down and prayed,

      (d) Father, if thou art willing, remove this cup from me; nevertheless not my will, but thine be done

    (c) And when he rose from prayer,

  (b) he came to the disciples and found them sleeping for sorrow;

(a) and he said to them, "Why do you sleep? Rise and pray that you may not enter into temptation."

Luke 22:40-46 (RSV), minus 43-44: "And there appeared to him an angel from heaven, strengthening him. And being in agony he prayed more earnestly; and his sweat became like great drops of blood falling down on the ground."

With the existence of literally hundreds of changes such as these in the texts, we see that rewriting history was apparently no big deal to ancient scribes.

With the advent of the Dead Sea Scrolls, however, and their dynamic of Qumran's "New Covenant in the Land of Damascus" versus the Gospel of Luke's "cup of the new testament in my blood, which is shed for you" (Luke 22:20b KJV), we must reconsider who is at work putting this in Luke. According to Dr. Eisenman, Paul was well aware of the Damascus Document and other Qumran writings, and would have been very interested in countering any derogatory allusions towards his positions on such a central issue as James' directives banning the consumption of blood. Paul, asserting that for him "all things are lawful" (1 Cor. 10:23) very cleverly twisted this Jamesian directive about "keeping the Temple [the body] pure" into a new theology about the necessity of ritual consumption of the Lord's "body" and "blood" which became the familiar Eucharist ritual of today. Whether Luke, as Paul's compatriot, personally installed this in his Gospel or not is an interesting question for Ehrman and Eisenman to perhaps debate. In any case, *it wasn't taught by any Master!* Perhaps it would be better to rely on the modern writings of more recent Masters in interpreting the message of a Master so long departed. Thankfully, such writings do exist. So there is really no need to guess at the intended meanings of archaic literary forms and vocabulary—we can see them in plainly written modern English, check with the texts in question, and be sure we have it right!

James Tabor is another researcher who is closing in on the truth. In his Jesus Dynasty, Tabor points out early Christians had a problem with John the Baptist being seen as an equal with Jesus. For example, it was not good to have one's sole Savior and king baptized by another. It made Jesus look inferior to need baptizing by John. So, the Gospels downplayed the role of John in various ways. Luke implied that he wasn't even involved since it happened after John was locked up (3:19-21). Matthew and Mark downplay John's baptism role. John's version doesn't specifically mention a baptism of Jesus. German scholars in the 19th century discovered the existence of Q ("Quelle"—German for "source") by subtracting material common to Matthew and Luke not found in their presumed prime source, Mark. What is left is 235 verses of "sayings" of Jesus. Like the Gospel of Thomas, another "sayings" record, Q obviously predates at least Matthew and Luke, so is more ancient and authentic as a source than even the Gospels. One subject in Q, as might be expected, is John the Baptist: Jesus asks the crowd what they went out into the wilderness (Dead Sea desert vicinity) to see. He answers for them, "'A prophet? Yes, I tell you, and more than a prophet.'" (Luke 7:26). Jesus then adds, "'I tell you, among those born of women none is greater than John.'" (7:28a). John, hence, is "greater" than, or the equal of, Jesus. What's interesting is the later, Christian scribal addition "yet he who is the least in the kingdom of God is greater than he" (7:28b)—more discomfort with equals to Christ. Original Matthew was in Hebrew. Hebrew Matthew has this from Jesus on

John, "'For all the prophets and the Law spoke *concerning* him,'" rather than the received Greek, "'for all the prophets and the Law spoke *until* him'" (11:13). Quoting Tabor, "Later Christians would be bothered by any words of Jesus that might imply John was a 'savior' rather than Jesus."

Familiar Q source materials to Bible readers include the Sermon on the Mount (Matthew 5-7) and Luke's Sermon on the Plain (Luke 6). Particularly noteworthy is the short letter of James, with, according to Tabor, over *thirty* references to Q sayings. These include "be doers of the word," "keep the whole Torah," "blessed are the poor," "woe to the rich," and "do not swear an oath." That Q and James have no trace of Pauline "justification by faith" or "atonement by the shed blood of Christ"—the heart and soul of Christian doctrine—is striking. The evidence is clear: The teachings of John, Jesus and James were not the teachings of Paul.

More dissembling is John 4:2. After Jesus hears the Pharisees heard he was baptizing he is said by Gospel writer John not to be baptizing—"only his disciples." This is after John the Baptist explicitly says he will (Matthew 3:11). This verse cannot be true. Again, Luke even tries to deny that Jesus was baptized by John in 3:19-21, having Jesus anonymously baptized after he was supposedly in prison.

Now for Daniel 7:27:

Most people don't know that in 382 CE, Pope Damasus commissioned accomplished linguist Jerome, the church historian at the time and his personal secretary, to undertake a new translation of the Bible from the Greek and Hebrew original, now known as the Vulgate, to replace the existing *Vetus Latina*. This translation shows an interesting change in the Vulgate derived King James Version compared to the Revised Standard Version—derived from the scholastically accepted, more faithful, Alexandrian Codex.

Daniel 7:27 KJV

And the kingdom and dominion, and the greatness of the kingdom under the whole heaven, shall be given to the people of the saints of the most High, whose kingdom is an everlasting kingdom, and all dominions shall serve and obey him.

Daniel 7:27 RSV

And the kingdom and the dominion and the greatness of the kingdoms under the whole heaven shall be given to the people of the saints of the Most High; their kingdom shall be an everlasting kingdom, and all dominions shall serve and obey them.

Notice the deleted gnostic language (dominion *to the people*—not God)? Do you think Pope Damasus might be involved? He commissioned the translation. And, incidentally, look at the *plural* "saints." These aren't Paul's "saints," as in "followers" in his letters, but "Masters" because "followers" don't have "people" (people *"of"* the saints)—only Masters or Saviors do! This, and the many allegorical Old Testament stories covered by other authors, below, show the Bible to be a mystic book of gnostic teachings. Ancient Judaism, from which Christianity sprang up, is itself a descendant of Zoroastrianism, with the addition of Christ as sacrificial lamb. Sacrifice, except that of a pure and consecrated life, was no part of the teaching of the Iranian Zarathustra, which the ancient Jews picked up from the Sumerians during one of their many periods of exile. The mystic Kabbalah tradition of Judaism finds its roots there.

Chapter Five

Selected Old Testament Parables

The Old Testament, whether history or fable, is full to brimming with mystic truth. The entire thing, when not genealogies or law-giving, is mystic allegory. Look no further than the story of Jonah. Perhaps no story in the Bible tests one's belief in the literal reading of it more than this fable of being swallowed by a big fish and emerging three days later to tell about it. The first clue comes as soon as verse 3 that there is more here than meets the eye. Jonah obviously had a special relationship with the Lord—but resisted Him. Jonah 1:1,3: "And *the word of the Lord* came to Jonah." "But Jonah rose to flee to Tarshish from the presence of the Lord." And just how does one do *that?* Isn't the Lord *everywhere?* In a word—no. As things in mystic translation would have it: The Lord ordered Jonah to go to Nineveh (v 2), but *he went the other way*—"*away* from the presence of the Lord" (v 3b). According to Dr. Randolph Stone, author of Mystic Bible, these cities are *symbols* of something much more spiritual and ethereal: "chakras," subtle, spiritual energy centers upon which one was, in that time, to work out one's enlightenment. We have already introduced the crown or "Kether" chakra in the discussion of the "single eye." The "whirling wheels" in the tenth chapter of Ezekiel are chakras. The cities in this story are subtle energy centers that animate the physical body and give us life. Through sustained concentration, a mystic practitioner can make some progress at opening his inner vision, even without a Master. Jonah was retreating from the Lord's presence, in the direction of "Nineveh"—the Manipura Chakra—by slipping to a lower energy center—the Swadishtana or Brahma Chakra, "Tarshish"—by way of "a ship"—the subtle energy current. In the Yogic System, the Brahma Chakra, always symbolized by a large water animal with a snout, has powerful currents, represented by "fishes," one upward and one downward. It was this downward, sensory, energy current that "swallowed up" Jonah for three days until the Lord heard his prayers (v 2:1) and released him. Jonah then "went to" Nineveh ("arising" on the current—v 3:2), so that "that great city" . . . "shall be overthrown" or conquered through his meditations. The "fasting" and repenting of the Nineveh residents in verses 3:5-10 represent the incomplete controlling of the fiery Manipura Chakra, so Jonah left it to "sit on the east side of the city" (v 4:5), the anterior—sensory—side of that energy center, and contemplate its completion. The "gourd" ("plant"—RSV) the Lord made to "shade" Jonah from his "grief" ("discomfort"—RSV) was to protect him from the heat developed by concentration on the fiery energy of the Manipura Chakra—center of digestive forces in the human body. To show Jonah he had not conquered the difficult chakra on his own (Jonah's "anger" of v 4:1) the Lord "appointed a worm" to destroy the gourd, and "it withered." When Jonah became aware of the heat again ("the sun rose"—v 4:8) Jonah repented and asked for relief. "It is better to die than to live." Because Jonah had doubted God's "Word," he was taught a severe lesson and did not "conquer Nineveh to live in it," but sat "outside of it," until—developing sufficient faith and trust in the Lord's help—he was able to "enter in" by subduing his mind and ego. *That* is the real story of Jonah. Is it any less believable than a "whale" vomiting a man (v 2:10) out on dry land *alive after three days* in its belly? The "feeding of the five thousand" in Luke 9:12-17 with "five loaves and two fishes" is a similar theme, told in the setting of feeding the multitude. The "loaves" are symbols of the chakras and the "fishes" the currents of subtle energy going in opposite directions in man, the groupings of fifty each being symbolic of the five senses and the twelve baskets of leftovers the abundance of God sufficient for the completion of man.

With miracle after miracle, the story of Exodus is either an allegory (whether based on historical fact or not) or the most extreme demonstration of the miraculous beyond all proportion to natural law—either before or since. From start to finish, this is the epic story of the soul's journey from sense bondage in desert Egypt, the land of the Pharaoh—the lower mind (indulgence, gluttony, the lower urges)—to the "Promised Land" of Canaan: union with the Lord in Spirit. Since the so-called "Holy Land" of "milk and honey" was pretty much desert, this storyline is allegorical. The people of Israel are the souls in "bondage" to the lower mind (Pharaoh) whose thoughts and actions—the Pharaoh's magicians and soothsayers—bind the souls to this world (Egypt). Moses, the higher mind, who is drawn from the River Nile of self-indulgence, leads his people out of bondage with the help of his brother and right-hand man, Aaron—the intellect or "buddhi"—eloquent speaker of the higher mind. Pharaoh's daughter, who saves Moses, typifies the motherly instinct in this "lower" sphere of action. The father-in-law of Moses represents the soul of Israel, absorbed with their interests and trying to guide Moses. With parallels in the visions of Daniel, and John (in Revelations), the Exodus is set over a vast time span as an epic tale of the evolution of man's soul. Pharoah's command to drown all male children of Israel (echoed in the reputed command of Herod centuries later to kill all young male children of Judea in an attempt to kill the Christ child) meant the soul had no chance to express its spiritual nature in the oppressive setting of sense indulgence called Egypt.

The infamous "serpent" of the Garden, and the "serpent" that came from the "rod" which Moses cast to the "ground" in Exodus 4:2 have nothing to do with reptiles. The serpent that beguiled Eve in Genesis 3:13 represents the coiled serpentine subtle energy called Kundalini in Eastern mysticism—known in the West as the "sex drive." That same energy is called the "serpent" in Exodus, which tempted Moses—but he "fled from it", taking it by the "tail" or base of the human spine and *transmuting it* from sexual energy into spiritual attainment (which, incidentally, is often indicated by reference to yielding a "male" child, as compared to a "female child," or failed attempt). Moses "caught" the serpent through concentration, and it "became a rod in his hand"—or a force to be used spiritually—and the "God of Abraham, Isaac, and Jacob appeared to him" (Exodus 4:4-5).

The shepherd's staff, or rod in the hands of Moses is a symbol, too, of course. Having the same symbolism as the wand of Mercury, or the Caduceus of Egypt and India, it represents the "sun and moon"

energies entwining the spinal column with the brain at the top
with the wings of the mind. One will find this clearly illustrated
as the sign of physicians of old as the "Staff of Caduceus." When
"cast to the ground" (v 3)—or used as sensory stimulation, the
energy becomes the tempter—the serpent—the very same serpent
which overcame Eve in the Garden. The shepherd's staff with its
crook well represents the energy flow from the Tisra Til (single
eye) up, backward, and down the spinal column energizing the
five chakras below, and animating the body. Moses, having been
given the power of the "Word," could handle the serpent by
taking it "by the tail." Moses thereby used the power under his
control to go back to "Egypt" and conquer the wayward mind
there. When Pharaoh's magicians (lower mind impulses) did
the same, Moses's staff became a snake that "swallowed" all the
others, i.e., he overcame these impulses by controlling his mind
(through meditation). The lesson of the "leprous hand" in Moses'
bosom, repaired by the Lord's command, is to show that of his
own will man's work is flawed, but in the service of the Lord,
it is good. The "water of the Nile" poured on "dry ground" (vv
6-7) is the vital force of the body wasted on the "red blood" of
bodily passions. All the plagues that visited "Pharaoh's Egypt" are
symbols of the human condition as well. The gnats (or lice) are
the misery of an unclean mind and body, flies breed the diseases
of impure living, death of cattle represent the destructive animal
passions, boils result from man's gluttony, hail and fire from the
sky are man's coldness of heart and destructive anger, raining
down everywhere except Goshen, where the Israelites happened
to be. Locusts are greed, darkness over the land is selfishness,
and the granddaddy of them all—the demand for the first-born,
sacrificed—is the ultimate surrender of the entire lower animal

nature, or "Self." The spiritual Path is not for the weak willed! Did you really think it was?

Therefore, the male child—successful attempt at spiritual effort—is sent out to the wilderness (the still and receptive mind) to practice devotion to God in Deuteronomy 10:12-11:32. "You shall therefore lay up *these words* [same as 'word'] of mine in your heart and in your soul [not your mind]; and you shall bind them as a sign upon your hand, *and they shall be as frontlets* [decoration, jewelry] *between your eyes* [i.e., the single eye!]" (Deut. 11:18). Can it get any clearer than that? Perhaps this from Revelation 22:4: "they shall see his face [in astral form], and *his name shall be on their foreheads.*" That immediately follows the showing of the vision of "the river of the water of life [the 'Word' or Holy Spirit], bright as crystal, flowing from the throne of God and of the Lamb [the Savior] through the middle of the street of the city [celestial Sahansdal Kanwal—holy 'Jerusalem' within, in spirit]." Incidentally, there is a key verse in Deuteronomy—verse 6:15—which is mistranslated in *both* the King James and the Revised Standard Versions. "For the Lord thy God is a jealous God *among you*; lest the anger of the Lord thy God be kindled against thee, and destroy thee from off the face of the earth" (KJV), and "for the Lord your God *in the midst of you* is a jealous God; lest the anger of the Lord your God be kindled against you, and he destroy you from off the face of the earth" (RSV). The correct version, as you may have guessed by now, is "*within you*"—the gnostic reality of the indwelling Spirit.

Shema Yisrael ("Hear, [O] Israel"), or just Shema, are "the first two words of a section of the Torah (Hebrew Bible) that is a centerpiece of the morning and evening Jewish prayer service [mitzvah]"

(Wikipedia). "Hear, O Israel, the Lord is our God, the Lord is One" (Deut. 6:4). Applied by extension to Deuteronomy 6:4-9, 11:13-21, and Numbers 15:37-41--the VaEtchannan, Eikev, and Schlach, respectively--it comprises the essence of Judaism. These are scriptures carefully placed in "tefillin" (leather boxes worn on the forehead), on "phylacteries" (leather arm banding), and on doorposts (cased parchment "mezuzot") as a way for the Orthodox Jewish faithful to practice their devotions, according to the Oral Torah. Phylacteries were found at Qumran, so the practice has a long history. "These *words,* which I command thee this day, shall be *in thy heart:* And thou shalt bind them [metaphorically!] for a sign upon thine hand, and they shall be as frontlets *between thine eyes"* (Deut. 6:6,8 KJV). The words are to be *frontlets* (decorations, jewelry, *'the Word')* for you--*in your heart,* and *between your eyes.* The mystic commandment here--Deuteronomy 6--is daily prayer (meditation) on "the Word ['words']" at the "single eye," as Yahweh commands. Through misunderstanding of the terms "words" and "kill" in Deuteronomy, the practitioners actually *break* two commandments: the second, "thou shalt make no likeness of any *thing* ['words or Word'] *that is in heaven,* and the sixth, "thou shalt not *kill* [animals, for their leather]."

In all mystic writings and discourses, the house usually signifies the human body. The Passover Lamb of Exodus 12:21-29 is symbolic, again, of the overcoming of the animal passions. The blood on the lintel (top or head) and posts (body, hands, and feet), is similar in type to the "seal *on their foreheads"* of Revelation 9:4, allowing the devotee to be spared. This key piece of salvation anatomy, the forehead, is also prominent in Ezekiel's vision of the Lord to "the man in linen with the inkhorn by his side"

(James?, 9:2). "And the Lord said unto him, Go through the midst of the city, through the midst of Jerusalem, and set a mark *upon the foreheads* of the men that sigh and and that cry for all the abominations that be done in the midst of the city" (v 9:4, KJV—interesting that this Ezekiel verse is the same verse number in Revelation to refer to it!). This would save them from the fate of the men, women, and children who were not true to his "Word" in claiming that the Lord "had forsaken the earth" (because they did not meditate upon Him) and "seeth [them] not" (v 9:9) who were to be slain *utterly* throughout the city (v 9:6). The slaying "utterly" here, as with most of the killing carried out by "the Lord" or his followers, in parables and visions such as these is actually referring to the natural death and rebirth of those in question. The Lord really isn't so bloodthirsty, it is all due to their karma. The final assault by Pharaoh on the beleaguered souls of Israel at Pihahiroth (chapter 14), between Migdol and the Red Sea (Is this the possible origin of "between the devil and the deep blue sea"—meaning "predicament"?) is thwarted by the "east wind" of the Lord (v 21)—the Sound Current, or "Word," which blew "all night" (in meditation!) and parted the waters (passions) allowing the faithful to go through "on dry land" to the inner regions of the spirit, the Pharaoh's warriors—those pesky lower desires—drowning behind them. Exodus 14:13-14: "And Moses said to the people, 'Fear not, stand firm, and see the salvation of the Lord, which will work for you today; for the Egyptians you see today you shall never see again. The Lord will fight for you, *and you only have to be still.*" The Pharaoh's "lower mind" charioteers drown in the watery grave of life's passions when subdued by the uplifting spiritual currents—the "pillar of fire" of life-force in the spinal column "rod of Moses"—*within the disciple.* You *"only have to be still"* in meditation at the single eye, the "narrow gate" of the soul, and fearlessly leave your body in mental concentration to "see the salvation of your Lord." Exodus 14:24 has an interesting allusion to "the morning watch" where the Lord looks down on the host of Egyptians "discomfiting them" and "clogging their chariot wheels so they drove heavily." Compare this with the whirling wheels or "charkras" in Ezekiel 1 to see the mental energy rechanneled in the disciple in "morning watch" or meditation (Matthew 26:40). "And the Egyptians [desire] said, 'Let us flee from before Israel [the believers]; for the Lord fights for them before the Egyptians'" (Ex. 14:25). The song Moses and his people sang in chapter 15 is their tribute to the "Word" of the Lord when "Thou didst blow with thy wind [of Spirit]" (v 10) and covered the pursuing lower-mind "Egyptians," "purchasing" the people (v 16) that He will "plant on [His] mountain" (v 17)—meaning "in His Spirit."

Other stories of the Old Testament are equally mystic in character. The "fall" of man didn't begin with Eve and her "apple." It actually happened when God "caused a deep sleep to fall upon" Adam in Genesis 2:21—a fall from the grace of His presence *in Spirit.* This was the creation of the "Adamic race" or "fallen" man so thoroughly covered in the gnostic gospels. The descent of man into physical bodies wasn't to happen *until after* the expulsion from the Garden, in Genesis 3:21: "And the Lord God made for Adam and for his wife garments of skins, and clothed them."—"skins" meaning *bodies*, not clothing. The "fall" was the lack of control of the desire body, represented by "woman"—which, men forget, was *a part of Adam* before "she" was "taken out of Man" (Gen. 2:23). When the desire is redirected in pursuit of God, the energy is put to good use—"he [man] shall bruise your head [the 'serpent's' lower desires]"—and the serpent "shall bruise his heel" (Gen. 3:15). "The three "trees" in the "Garden" of the body (Gen. 2:9) are the three "gunas" or "energies" of the Vedas. "The Tree of Life" is the airy "Tattwa" or active guna in man, "the Tree of Knowledge of Good and Evil" is the regenerative, watery Tattwa associated with reproduction and sexual pleasure, which alone among all animals can be used to either advance or degenerate the individual depending on how it is used and the "Trees Good for Food" are the fiery energies of digestion mentioned above as the Manipura chakra. These three most active Tattwas convey the essence of the three "gunas" throughout the human body as breath, blood, and nourishment—or air, water, and fire substance, all ultimately producing the physical body. Noah's Ark is representative of God ferrying the righteous across the "waters" of the above mentioned generative guna, the many animals in Noah's charge being the "animal nature" of that Tattwa. This story is obviously allegorical: it isn't likely that *all* animal types will fit in a three-hundred-cubit boat, especially without eating one another!

Perhaps there is no more famous allegorical story in the Bible than that of a young man named David and the Philistine Goliath, of Gath. Challenging King Saul and "the men of Israel" to send forward one man to do battle (1 Sam. 17:1-11) to see who will be "servant" to whom, the fearsome Goliath, "six cubits and a span" tall and clad in a bronze helmet and a coat of mail weighing "five thousand shecklels of bronze," descended to the valley between the two camps to await his challenger. Gathering "five smooth stones from the brook" with his "staff in his hands" (v 40) David refused the armor Saul had tried to give him (representing the

"armor" of the worldly man, "for I am not used to them," v 39),
and went forward to meet Goliath at the battle line. We all know
how it turned out. With the first stone he sent flying toward
Goliath from his sling it was all over. The stone hit the giant
squarely *in the forehead* and killed him. David then took Goliath's
own sword, "for he had none," and cut off his head with it (vv
48-51) scattering the onlooking Philistines. The "five smooth
stones" are *the five holy names* of the Lord—actually, "Archons" or
etherial rulers of the five inner regions—repeated by the righteous
David in his devotions, one after the other, *at the center of the
forehead*—the single eye of Matthew 6:22 and countless other
similar passages—which slew the Goliath ego-self in the young
David, holy beyond his years. That David went into battle with
only the sling and his staff and used Goliath's own sword to "cut
off his head" shows that the Lord's "name" alone (v 45), when
raised up "the staff" of the subtle spiritual body is sufficient to
us to overcome our lower natures, as it was for Moses as we saw
earlier. Beloved by all Israel and Judah (v 18:16) David went on
to further success in all his undertakings (v 18:14).

Elsewhere, Joshua fought and slew the "five kings"—lust, anger
greed, attachment, and vanity—in Joshua 10:16-28. This he
accomplished with his victorious concentration on the inner
(Astral) sun and moon in the Valleys of "Gibeon [the sun] and
Aijalon [the moon]." It is mental concentration that made them
"stand still" (Josh. 10:12-13) within Joshua's inner sight. The fall
of Jericho in chapter six is the story of conquering the ego of Self
at the gate of the "Promised Land." The "spies" sent by Joshua to
the city (v 6:22) and saved by the Harlot Rahob are the two energy
currents of consciousness. Jericho is Joshua's self-identity. Rahob

represents the regenerative impulse, situated on "the wall"—the rim of the pelvis. When the faithful circled the city and on the seventh day shouted in unison (Joshua's concentrated meditation) the walls fell, the "ego" of Jericho was killed, and the regenerative impulse was relieved of suppression and need not play harlot any longer—the center was conquered. Rahob—regenerative energy now transmuted into higher consciousness—no longer bound by her oath to "stay in her house" of the body until the two spies "came for her" (the two energy currents taking the life force upward) served Joshua well, and was rewarded: "and her father's household, and all who belonged to her [his regenerative abilities], Joshua saved alive; and she dwelt in Israel [to properly perpetuate the race] to this day"—verse 6:25. Is there a better explanation for the shouting down of solid rock walls?

Another example of mystic storytelling is the mystic, Balaam, and the ass. Balaam (our old "Devil" code word), prophet of Bel, was being prevailed upon by King Balak of Moab to curse the Israelites in his struggle with them, as he was known to be an accomplished Seer of great power. Obeying the Lord, Balaam refused the many gifts offered by Balak (Num. 22:7-18). Wanting to demonstrate his loyalty to the king, and receiving God's permission, Balaam finally agreed to go. Here's where the fun starts. In Numbers 22:23-40, the ass on which Balaam was riding "saw the angel of the Lord standing in the road, with a drawn sword in his hand." The ass turned aside, and Balaam "struck" it. The ass again saw the angel "in a narrow path between the vineyards," walled on either side. Pressing Balaam's foot against the wall, the ass gets smacked again. The third time the angel blocked Balaam's way, with no where for the ass to turn, she lay down and the Lord "opened the mouth" of the ass: "What have I done to you that you have struck me these three times?" (v 28). "And Balaam said to the ass, 'Because you have made sport of me. I wish I had a sword in my hand for then I would have killed you.'" The Lord then "opened the eyes" of Balaam, who had "fallen on his face" (v 31), and he saw the angel standing in the way with sword drawn. Balaam realizes he was about to disobey the Lord and repents. The ass represents the individual mind of the disciple, which, through much training and discipline tried to stop the unwary Balaam from making a mistake but couldn't. While en route to the king, the Lord blocked the way because Balaam had put the lesser cause (loyalty to the king) before the greater (obedience to God). Three times Balaam failed to recognize and acknowledge his own achievements in spiritual development before the Lord rewarded him and "opened his eye[s]" to his "higher mind." The story isn't about talking animals, but "seeing" within. This is the same Balaam who later has his "eye" [singular] opened upon "hearing the word[s] of God" (Num. 24:3), having his "eyes uncovered" (v 16) and then being given the famous "Star prophecy" (vv 17-19), which, cited at least three times in the Qumran corpus, is, together with the Isaiah 11:1-5 "shoot from the stump of Jesse" prophecy, given as the cause for the Jewish revolt against Rome in the mid-first century CE, according to Dr. Eisenman. (This puts a later date on the Dead Sea Scrolls than first assigned, and helps identify James as successor to Jesus, among other things.) Balaam later angers God by promoting idolatry (hence the B-L-A "devil" code word connection).

In the Book of Job, chapter 19 (RSV):

[25] "For I know that my Redeemer lives,
and at last he will stand upon the earth;*
[26] and after my skin has been thus destroyed,
then from* my flesh I shall see God,
[27] whom I shall see on my side,*
and my eyes shall behold, and not another.
My heart faints within me!"

*In this passage from Job, the three words "earth," "from," and "on my side" have footnotes reading "or dust," "or without," and "or for myself," which, when all are substituted in their respective places, now reads:

[25] "For I know that my Redeemer lives,
and at last he will *stand upon the dust*;
[26] and after my skin has been thus destroyed,
then *without my flesh* I shall see God,
[27] whom I shall *see for myself*
and my eyes shall behold, and not another.
My heart faints within me."

"Dust" is the human form (Gen. 3:19) where the Redeemer will "stand." Thus is the "skin" or ego, destroyed, and the soul will "see" God, by transcending the "flesh" of the human body, and beholding "no other"—the self that has been destroyed by mystic union with God. Now the passage not only finally makes sense, it reveals its poetic beauty as well.

A final note about this passage from Job is the KJV mistranslation "in my flesh"—worse than the RSV "from my flesh"—which should be "without my flesh", the *exact opposite* meaning intended. This, of course, suited an early church conception of a physical resurrection, which we know to be a wrong conception from John 11:25 and the Gospel of Philip, both showing a *living* resurrection of the spirit.

Psalm 22—"Like a Lion":

(From Vridar.wordpress.com, edited): It is an axiom among fundamentalists and even many mainstream conservative Christians that Psalm 22 contains an incontrovertible prophecy of the crucifixion of Jesus, and that the key verse establishing this "fact" is the one that reads "They pierced my hands and my feet." (v 22:16). There is no doubt that two of the gospel authors took the first verse of this Psalm "My God, my God, why have you forsaken me?" and placed it in the mouth of Jesus on the cross. All four gospels used the 18th verse too, which says, "They divide my garments among them, and for my clothing they cast lots." And one drew on the mocking: "All those who see me laugh me to scorn . . . saying, 'He trusted in the Lord, let him rescue him, let him deliver him, since he delights in him!'" (vv 22:7-8). All of these verses are found in the gospels as part of the crucifixion scene: "And when they crucified him, they divided his garments, casting lots for them" (Mark 15:24; Matthew 27:35; Luke 23:34; John 19:24). "And at the ninth hour Jesus cried out with a loud voice, saying, " . . . 'My God, my God, why have you forsaken me?'" (Mark 15:34; Matt 27:46). "Likewise the chief priests, also mocking with the scribes and elders, said 'He trusted in God; let him deliver him now if he will have him'" (Matthew 27:41-43).

Is it not strange that the verse in that same Psalm that says "they pierced my hands and my feet" should not be used at all in any of the gospels? This verse, after all, is the one singular verse that would establish that it is speaking, at the very least metaphorically, of a crucifixion. Yet it is totally absent from the gospels. There is not even any narrative detail that makes special mention of nails going through the hands and feet of Jesus at the time he is being crucified. (The closest any gospel comes to this is at the time of the resurrection when Thomas refers to nail-prints in Jesus' hands. But there is no mention of it in the Psalm.)

But one might as well ask, is it not strange that the Psalm spoke of hands and feet being pierced (presumably a crucifixion image) at all? Such a verse does not sit well at all with the rest of the Psalm. The psalmist begins with a cry to God and a complaint that he has been uttering that cry for days and nights without an answer: "My God, my God, why have you forsaken me? . . . I cry in the daytime, but you do not hear; *And in the night season* [meditation!—italics mine], and am not silent." (vv 22:1-2). Jesus was not on the cross for days and nights, and the Gospel of Luke informs us that God certainly heard the prayer Jesus uttered the previous night. He sent an angel to help bolster his courage. Yet this Psalm opens with a cry that is the desperation felt from having no answer for, at the very least, a whole day and night. This cannot be reconciled with the crucifixion scene of the gospels.

Then there is the verse that says the psalmist was attached to God from the time of his birth: "From my mother's womb you have been my God." (v 22:10). That surely must raise some eyebrows among those who believe that Jesus was, and knew he was, part of the godhead from eternity. But it gets worse for those who assume this Psalm is depicting a man on a cross. "Be not far from me, for trouble is near" (v 22:11). A person nailed to a wooden stake to die a slow agonizing death cries out, "I see trouble up ahead"? Now that is an optimist. Always thinking that no matter how bad the present situation is it could always be worse. "Please God, I can handle you deserting me at this moment, but I do hope you hurry up and come to help me when I'm in real trouble!"

Then there is that strange plea to be saved from the sword! "Deliver me from the sword" (v 22:20). Always worth remembering to ask God to deliver you from a sword when he lets you experience the inconvenience of being crucified! So the broader context of the Psalm speaks against it being a foretelling of a crucifixion, but there is metaphoric imagery throughout that also needs to be appreciated to understand it fully. Wild animal imagery dominates: "Many bulls encompass me; strong bulls of Bashan surround me. They open wide their ~~their~~ mouths at me, like a ravening and roaring lion" (vv 12-13). "Yea, dogs are round about me; a company of evildoers encircle me" (v 16). "Deliver my soul from the power of the sword, my life from the power of the dog. Save me from the mouth of the lion, my afflicted soul from the horns of the wild oxen!" (vv 20-21). It is not surprising therefore to find that the Hebrew Bible contains a passage with the same wild lion imagery that happens to be missing from a Greek text of this Psalm that was preserved and copied by a later generation of Christians: "Like a lion they are at my hands and my feet." In place of this Hebrew verse the Greek translation of this Psalm (which has been the work of Christian, not Hebrew, scribes) reads: "They pierced my hands and my feet." "Pierce" has replaced "like a lion". King David used the word "kaari" which is Hebrew for "like a lion"—not "pierced". "Pierced" would have been "daqar" or "ratza"—common Hebrew words found elsewhere in Jewish scriptures. This same word "kaari" is, elsewhere, in scripture translated correctly (Isaiah 38:13), so it's not like the Christian translators didn't know. Earliest known evidence of this change is mid-second century Justin Martyr in Dialogue of Trypho, so it appears to be solely the work of Christian scribes. (see: mechon-mamre.org for Hebrew/English translation of Psalm 22 text)

This is presented here not to show how prophecy is falsified, as it may—or may not—be a foretelling of Jesus as Christ (It doesn't mean he was the only one!) but the fact that texts have been altered, along with gospel writers embellishing their narratives to fit their needs, shows how stories can be self-generated. An exhaustive examination of scripture with this in mind would be most interesting indeed.

Bishop Spong's Resurrection: Myth or Reality? discusses a fascinating angle on prophecy fulfillment through the ancient Hebraic storytelling process called "midrash." For a thorough examination, the reader is urged to read his account, but for our purposes, it is simply pointed out that what may seem prophetic fulfillment is in reality a form of recycled storytelling. Midrash is of three types: Halakha, Haggadah, and Pesiqta. Halakha is an interpretation of the law of the Torah. Haggadah is the interpretation of a story or an event by relating it to another story or event in sacred history. Pesiqta is a sermon or an exhortation written midrashically to capture themes of the past to enable them to be seen as operative in the present. Haggadah and Pesiqta are what we see in the Gospel stories of the life of Jesus. It isn't that the events themselves recur, but that the religious tradition of the Jewish people (who in turn received their tradition from Egyptian religious tradition) demands that there be continuity with the past, and drives the telling of the story. According to Bishop Spong, details about how stories of some events were related are difficult to figure out without resorting to the method of midrash: Take, for example, the birth in the manger (Luke 2); the temptation in the wilderness (Matthew 4 and Luke 4); Joseph's dream inspired flight to Egypt to avoid the slaughter of the innocents (Matthew 2); the content of the Gethsemane prayer (Luke 22) when Jesus went "a stone's throw away from the others" (Luke 22:41) and they were all asleep when he returned and was quickly arrested; and what Jesus said on the cross, what the crowd said, what the other two on their crosses said, and what the centurion said (Luke 23), all after his entourage had all fled. Who recorded all these comments? Who transmitted them? We are told what the soldiers did, what Pilate did, what Herod did, and what Simon of Cyrene did. Did any of these submit transcripts to the Gospel writers? (Thinking Psalm 22? Starting to make sense now? These stories are remakes from ancient Judaic myths.)

What appears to be prophecy can be simply storytelling by those very familiar with the tomes of their past and wanting to keep tradition alive. Just as Moses parted the sea, and Joshua parted the River Jordan, the tale of God's new standard bearer has Jesus parting not the river he was "baptized" in, but the heavens themselves, as if to emphasize that this is the expected Messiah. This, however, was hardly new either. Elijah (2 Kings 2:7-8) and Elisha (2 Kings 2:14) were also adept at "parting the waters." Seems like nobody liked getting their feet wet back then! For Jesus to have both fulfilled, and expanded the Jewish tradition, the Gospel writers not only had him part the heavens, but had the waters of life flow right out of people: "If anyone thirst, let him come unto me and drink. He who believes in me, as the scripture has said, 'Out of his heart shall flow rivers of living water'" (John 7:39). The story of the guiding star (which is actually a spiritual, "star"-like light, seen within) had appeared in earlier midrashic tradition in the stories of the birth of Abraham, Isaac, and even of Moses. Childless Zechariah and Elizabeth is a retelling of the story of Abraham and Sarah, similarly childless. And the very birth of Jesus in Bethlehem (Luke 2, Matthew 2), whose family is there for the census and tax enrollment of Quirinius (now believed to be some ten years after Jesus's birth), is not well explained for a family from Nazareth traveling a hundred hard miles with a woman expecting birth, who was not even allowed to own taxable property! Matthew had to get the family back to Nazareth (v 2:23) to fulfill the "prophecy of the Nazarene"—which is itself nowhere to be found in the scripture except in an obscure reference to a "stem [the root word in Hebrew for Nazarene]" of Jesse in Isaiah 11:1. So Joseph has the family go back to Israel from Egypt (v 2:21) after an angel warned Joseph that "those who sought the child's life" had died (Herod, v 2:20) because Judea was now ruled by Herod's son Archelaus, who so scared him (*more* than Herod?) as to send him to Nazareth (if there even was such a town), to the district Galilee (v 2:22), and not Bethlehem! Then we go on to the forty days and nights tempted in the wilderness by the devil who wants Jesus to make bread from stones in the desert (Matthew 4:3-4) which we have seen before (Deut. 8:2-3: "forty" years, and "eating manna in the wilderness"). It's a wonder *anything* written about the life of Jesus Christ is believed! This was all done as the way to extend and link the mythic tradition of the forefathers to the present and validate Jesus as the new expression of God in the ongoing story of "God's people," the Jews.

Conclusion

The true message of Jesus Christ was one of non-sacrificial, individual, mystic salvation—*spoken to his own—and for his time only.* The untrue message about Jesus Christ is that he came as sole universal sacrificial Savior to die as a payment for the sins of everyone who ever lived, or would ever live, in the world. Jesus was a Savior, his Master and cousin, John the Baptist, was also a Savior, and his successor and brother, James the Just, was another Savior—or Master—as they have also been called. All three brought the exact same message of mystic soul liberation, all three possessed the same power to carry it out. All three unfortunately paid with their lives to bring the truth of this spiritual liberation to a troubled world. More research is needed, but it appears likely that Jesus' other two brothers, Theudas and Simeon bar Cleophas were likewise both Masters and martyrs. There have been *hundreds* of Saviors, some having come before Jesus, many having come since Jesus.

Jesus probably saved hundreds of people, but not by his having been crucified. The cross of crucifixion is not a symbol of salvation. It is a symbol of cruelty. It could perhaps be said it is a symbol of submission, but never—*ever*—a symbol of salvation. Many other Saviors have died as martyrs, not just Christ alone. Vicarious atonement is only partially true according to the Masters as disciples still undergo some karma even after their initiation, so the Master need not die to convey salvation—and that most certainly not for those generations of other times.

Tunnel vision is an insidious malady. People can hold a false belief for so long, especially when so many others also before them believed wrongly, that they discard, to their detriment, *new facts* which counter their wrong beliefs simply because they don't fit with their preconceptions. No one likes admitting that one is wrong. But in the face of evidence to the contrary, this isn't rational thinking. Just because someone hears something a million times doesn't make it so—it could be *wrong* a million times. The evidence of a systematic skewing of the original teachings of Jesus Christ is overwhelming and clear. Whether intentional or unintentional—and it is both—matters not. What matters is that the evidence is indisputable, abundant, and permanent. It should be universally acknowledged as such.

The Bible is great literature. It is not so great an instruction manual. Paul's teachings in his letters and the book of Acts amounted to a "New Testament" all right—a "New Covenant" (the terms are identical in Greek) all his own that was to fly in the face of scripture: "*What has been is what will be, and what has been done is what will be done; and there is nothing new under the sun*" (Eccles. 1:9). If his authority, derived only from a self-professed vision of the Lord Jesus, was to be his basis for taking control of the church why is it he never even mentions the event, so life-changing as it was supposed to have been? Perhaps even he knew how specious it was. This he leaves to Luke. Paul tried to institute a new method of salvation that wasn't Jesus' and James' "justification by works and faith" (Jas. 2:14-26) but one of "the righteousness from

God which depends on faith" (Gal. 2:16, Phil. 3:9). If faith alone is what is so important for salvation, why is that *never mentioned* in the Synoptics? Why is "continues to see, continues believing" absent from John? This was his own invention born from expanding Habakkuk 2:4 ("the righteous shall live by his faith") into a whole new religion. The world was forever changed—but, unfortunately, often not for the better. And it wasn't until nineteen hundred years later—right now—with the advent of the Qumran Dead Sea Scrolls and Nag Hammadi Library discoveries that the story could finally be rightly and fully told. The present situation doesn't call for assigning blame or responsibility, except where blatant obstruction of dissemination of new materials, for whatever reason, is uncovered, such as evidently occurred with the Dead Sea Scrolls until just recently. This has been thoroughly covered in various different works, several listed below. We can all be thankful, on the other hand, that we now have these new sources and should strive to make the most of them.

Even before the Gospels introduce us to Jesus Christ by way of "an angel of the Lord" in Matthew 1:21, we learn from his genealogy that he is "the son of David, the son of Abraham" (Matthew 1:1). When David was to pass on, the Lord declared to David that He would "make a house for him." "When your days are fulfilled and you lie down with your fathers, I will raise up your offspring after you, who shall come forth from your body and I will establish his kingdom. He shall build a house *for my name*, and I will establish *the throne* of his kingdom *forever*" (2 Sam. 7:11-13). This has caused huge troubles. Whether Abraham's or David's "seed" have physical, genetic descendants or not, this passage, as with others of like verbiage, obviously refers to a heavenly kingdom, since worldly ones all perish. (Is it really necessary to point that out?) The "name" is *God's Name*—the "Word" or

Voice of the Lord, or any of a thousand other names given It. The "throne" of his kingdom is at the "single eye" *within each of us* and the "nation" of Israel He rules over is the nation *of the chosen* of God, not merely the "Israelites." The words of the Hebrew prophets are fulfilled whenever a Christ or Messiah *sits on his "throne" within those chosen ones* in the "last days" of their lives to be "resurrected" at that time, as He so wills. God hasn't excluded everyone who isn't an Israeli or Jew (or Christian, either!) from the kingdom. His is a dominion that extends *over everyone.* Jesus confirmed this in Matthew 8:11-12a: "I tell you, many will come from east and west and sit at table with Abraham, Isaac, and Jacob in the kingdom of heaven, while the sons of the kingdom will be thrown into outer darkness." The "covenant" that the Lord affirms He established in Jeremiah 33:25 is with "*day and night,*" and "the ordinances of *heaven and earth,*" not just the descendants of Jacob and David. Day and night, and heaven and earth are mine just as much as they are the "seed" of Abraham, Isaac, or Jacob. These lines must be read *as literature,* not law!

The War Scroll, 1QM (*Milhamah* is Hebrew for "war"), found in Cave 1 at Qumran, and in fragments in Cave 4, ironically one of the first seven scrolls recovered by Bedouin herdsmen, with such obviously archetypal elements as protagonist Israel, "The Sons of Light", and the "Kittim" Romans, "The Sons of Darkness", engaged in pitched battle with the forces of "Belial" (the Devil) after the Sons of Light return from the Wilderness of the Peoples desert Camps (Qumran) to the Wilderness of Jerusalem, is pure metaphor. The *seven* battles of the *twelve* tribes, with *seven* engagements, *seven* infantry formations with *seven* stylized banners obviously is intended to have a better outcome (15:4-18:8) than the real Jewish War with the Romans in 66-70 CE with its disastrous outcome for Israel. This is a battle *in heaven* within the individual devotee: "Cursed is Belial for his contentious purpose, and accursed for his reprehensible rule." It was never intended to represent *anything* in this world. "The God of Israel is raising His hand in His wondrous strength against all the spirits of wickedness." Read more: http://meta-religion.com/World_Religions/Christianity/Other_Books/Dead_Sea_Scrolls/the_war_scroll.htm#ixzz0RrAVdwSZ

It must be kept in mind that Jesus never wrote anything—at least nothing we have found. He made no attempt to preserve his teachings for posterity, or to guard against their corruption. It is evident from the gnostic gospels that much of what he taught, he taught in secret, to a small group of select disciples, his famous discourses being meant for the consumption of the more general audience. If Jesus had intended to start a religion he certainly would have made better provision for the recording and preservation of his teachings. Although little information exists of Jesus in the written record independent of the New Testament, there is passing mention of him in the writings of a few historians of the time, such as Josephus. If he had wanted his teachings to be the central passage for mankind to the presence of the Divine, it would not have been particularly difficult for him to see to it personally. The intentional rewriting of history having now come fully to light, as well as the many changes in the manuscripts underlying the books that have come down to us, both intentional and mistaken, must be seen for what they are—a corruption of the original, mystic message of Jesus Christ. We must conclude that unlike Paul, Jesus never intended to start a religion—what to say of a corrupted one—or even to pass on so much as a greeting to the generations that either preceded or followed him.

The foregoing quotes of Jesus Christ, all spoken or created to be representations of his spoken words—never written—taken one at a time, may or may not be conclusive proof: but any two, three, or four—not to mention the dozens—given (and there are more) show Jesus' ministry to be a limited one indeed. He is telling *his* disciples what they need to hear. *You* are simply eavesdropping. Anyone saying "Now you know the Father because you have seen Him!" (paraphrasing John 14:7) must be speaking to a live audience. The logically correct reading of the John prologue (John 1:1-18) showing the salvific power of John the Baptist, attention to the implications of verses 36 and 40 in the "bread of life" discourse in John 6:35-40, the clear suggestion of *other* Masters in John 9:4-5, the straightforward declaration of task completion *while living* in the High Priestly Prayer (John chapter 17), and the rediscovery of the rightful place of James yield the unassailable conclusion that (1) Christ wasn't the first or last of his kind, (2) He had a time-limited ministry, and (3) He finished his mission two thousand years ago. In fact, just one verse, John 6:40 "For this is the will of my Father, that every one *who sees the Son* and believes in him should have eternal life; and I will raise him up at the last day"—read in context with John 6:36, as it should be—constitutes undeniable *proof* that Jesus taught a doctrine of exclusively contemporaneous Mastership. Anyone wishing to take issue with the thrust of this treatise must be prepared to offer an acceptable alternative explanation for what Jesus might have meant by saying that—of course, assuming he said it at all. We have apostles (Matthew 4:19, 11:11, 11:14, 16:19, 17:11, and John's many verses above), prophets (Exod. 33:17, 2 Kings 2:13, John 3:32), and angels (Matthew 1:21, Luke 2:11, Dan. 7:27), all indicating other Saviors, with Christ himself telling us so. You've been reading about other Masters all along—you just haven't noticed!

The demotion of John the Baptist from full equal Savior to Jesus Christ in Matthew's original Hebrew is matched only by the incredibly sophisticated minimizing and overwriting of James in the Lukan corpus. Comparing Shem Tov's reported Hebrew version of Matthew with the received Greek version yields the inescapable conclusion that the observed changes are consistent with other similar changes in the New Testament collection: always *away from a reading of the exalted status of other Masters* such as John the Baptist and James and *toward* that of one with *only* Jesus Christ as Savior. This isn't coincidental, but intentional. How could it be otherwise?

Jesus Christ said one must see and believe in him to be saved (John 6:40). Paul said to "confess his name" with the tongue "and believe in the heart" to be saved (Rom. 10:10). Jesus Christ was a Master. Paul never met him. Who should one believe? James said faith apart from works is "barren" (James 2:20). Paul said "the righteous shall live by faith" (Gal. 3:11). James was a Master. Paul tried to kill him (per Eisenman). Who should one believe? Is this *really* Christianity? Why not call it what it is? Paulianity!

Douglas Del Tondo: "Somewhere along the way commentators learned the power of repetition. They realized that if you repeat often enough an alleged truth about Christianity from Paul that is actually contrary to what Jesus says, you can create a social pressure to affix Paul's teaching upon Jesus Christ's teaching. This works because the listener recognizes Paul's teaching. The Christian is trained to ignore, however, that there is a mismatch between the words of Paul and Jesus. The repetition of Paul's doctrine serves to thwart Jesus' teaching every time. This wears down the Christian's critical sense to *understand the clear meaning of words* [italics his]. The Christian who is barraged by the drum-beat of *salvation by faith alone* [italics his] no longer senses the contradiction by Paul of Jesus. Any person free from this barrage can easily read Jesus' words and see the linguistic impossibility that both Paul and Jesus are saying the same thing." "Understanding the clear meaning of words" of Jesus as regards Paul's wayward teaching is important, but it extends further still. Jesus told us himself his ministry was finished (John 17:4). We should regard his word accordingly.

The concepts expounded here can be found time and again in the spiritual literature of all religions, and—as mankind's birthright—are as ancient as man himself. The mistake Christians have made (and that includes this writer as a teenager) is using someone—Paul—who didn't know a Master (he was always at odds with the one he could have known: James), never grasped what it is to be truly spiritual and had motives all his own, to wrongly interpret something—the Gospels—that they could never have understood properly in the first place, with all the duplicity and scribal obfuscations. How could they? With two thousand years to corrupt an oral history of (it is presumed) eyewitnesses, written generations after the events *by people* (not God) with agendas of their own, repeatedly transcribed (sometimes ten or twenty times!) by more people with more agenda and proven to be given to forgery, and finally translated one, two, or three times, it is a wonder there is anything *at all* left of Jesus' original teachings! Finally, Christians confound what they read with a misinterpretation of the mystic truth to the point where the real message of Christ is completely lost. However, it is the contention of this writer that, within a decade, it will be widely accepted that Paul, the main doctrinal figure in the New Testament, is totally discredited. He will be acknowledged as the perpetrator of the greatest fraud in all history when exposed for what he truly was: a Herodian insider, tortured by personal demons, bitterly resentful, a brilliant inventor of visions and intricate fictions perhaps unrivaled in literature. He will be seen as a man driven by an agenda all his own and in no way given to the uplift or salvation of anyone. As Dr. Eisenman puts it: "All of this is the most clever (albeit at times somewhat facile) verbal polemics and, to reiterate, it is not surprising it has both captivated and dazzled generations of adherents and all-too-easily overawed well-meaning and believing, yet rhetorically-unskilled, partisans ever since. These matters are certainly as complex as they are recondite, a fact working to the advantage of those during the last nineteen centuries who would attempt to simplify them." It is only too bad that it took so many centuries for the truth to come out. But come out it has. The Nag Hammadi books and Dead Sea Scrolls are not going to go away. The rewriting of *the real story* of Jesus and his family has begun. Dr. Eisenman has put us well down the road to understanding just what happened two thousand years ago that so shaped—and still shapes—our world. Beyond his rehabilitation of "the Righteous Teacher" James and the exposing of the "Spouter of Lying" Paul, recognizing the recurring incarnations of Divinity and the practical method of spiritual union these Masters bring is the only missing link to a final apprehension of the *true* story of Jesus Christ.

While the massive amount of new information and insight Dr. Eisenman brings to this endeavor will be difficult for many to assimilate, the confirmation of its veracity is present in the parallel details within other mystic traditions, most notably the evidence for serial Mastership, and emphasis on the "Word" of the Teacher and avoiding "pollution of the Temple," which this writer believes refers to the human body, and is fundamentally rooted in Jamesian strictures on personal consumption of animal foods and alcohol, and immoral behavior (e.g., fornication and incest)—all restraints constant in true spiritual traditions everywhere. This is a call for all who care about spiritual truth to come together in an appreciation of the underlying commonality of all these great traditions in mystic teaching. The advent of this new information is especially good news for our Jewish friends. They are forever absolved of blame for Christ's death. As brought to us by real historians such as Josephus and Hegesippus, his was a political—not religious—execution, by the occupying Romans, *no matter what the Gospels may say about it.* John's account goes to great lengths to try to pin his guilty verdict on the Jews, not Pilate, in John 19:12: "Upon this [Jesus telling Pilate he has no power unless given from God, v 11] Pilate sought to release him but the Jews cried out, 'If you release this man, you are not Caesar's friend; everyone who makes himself a king sets himself against Caesar.'" Only Romans crucified in first-century Palestine.

The Holy Bible is a diverse collection of often beautifully written works expressing the timeless truths of mysticism— the direct experience of the divine, here and now. Revealing passages about the mystic truth abound throughout the Bible, and could—and do—fill whole books. That's just the Bible—apocryphal books are even more revealing. Encouraging developments in this field include increasing recognition of the authenticity of Hebrew Matthew. More can found at http://www.shemtov.org/ These are exciting times in this field, and it is surely time gnostic spiritual literature was given its rightful place beside the other scriptures of the Holy Bible. Many good commentators are coming to the fore in the debate over the historic Jesus. Several of these are prominently placed in this work. However, there is certainly room for a much better representation of Eastern religious thought in the training in our divinity schools. This is a lamentable and glaring omission. There is, and has been, much misinformation—even disinformation—in religious commentary and the only antidote is reading widely and learning. Summing up his commentary section of Misquoting Jesus, Bart Ehrman says "What we need most in religious discussion is a frank and brutally honest sharing of views, not simply an insistence that everyone comes to believe, or disbelieve, as we do." It is hoped that this work makes such a contribution to better understanding of these scriptures.

The Masters themselves provide the criteria for recognizing a true Master (from The Path of the Masters, by Dr. Julian Johnson):

1) Masters are always vegetarian.
2) Masters never boast of their Mastership. They themselves will have their own Master who duly appoints the successor.
3) Masters never complain about their treatment at the hands of others.
4) Masters never find fault or blame others.
5) Masters never punish anyone. They leave that to the Negative Power (Kal or Devil).
6) Masters never do ascetic practices or perform austerities.
7) Masters are self-sustaining. They never beg or accept charity. They never sell their services.
8) Masters never perform miracles for public exhibition or to gain disciples.
9) Masters teach, practice, and initiate into, what today is called in India Surat Shabd Yoga.
10) Masters identify the highest levels of the five higher realms by light and by sound emanations.

Well-known Masters of the past include the Judaic: Seth, Noah, Moses, Jacob, David, Elijah, Elisha, Melchizedek, and John the Baptist, Jesus, and James; and the Muslim (Islamic Masters are called Murshad or Murshid): Bulleh Shah, Sarmad, Maulana Rum, Muhammad, and Shamas-i-Tabriz; Guru Nanak and his nine Sikh successors; Hindus Dadu, Paltu, Namdev, Kabir, Tukaram, Ravidas, and Mirabai (a woman); Mani, Buddha, Zarathustra, and more recently: Tulsi Sahib.

The three Abrahamic religions: Judaism (14 million adherents), Christianity (2.1 billion), and Islam (1.5 billion), have salvation doctrine which is at odds with each other and the teachings of their own central characters. The Jews are still looking for a Messiah, Christians believe theirs is the One and Only, and Muslims claim a final prophet. If they all claim to worship one Supreme Being and their teachings differ, at least two must be false—or all three. Before these three religions (fully half the world's population) actually usher in the wrongly construed "end of days," perhaps in a religious war begun by mistake (The Jews and some Christians eagerly await a rebuilt Temple on the site of the Islamic "Dome of the Rock" and then "the Messiah" or Jesus will come!), we should all take the time to become fully educated. The frictions between these three groups, and between them and the world at large, are all a tragic mistake—a misreading of the "scriptures." The visions and stories of scripture are *figurative! They are not to be read literally.* These are not *real* stories of mythic giants, talking animals, whales that harbor living humans, the parting of seas and rivers, or a man who saved others from hell by being tortured to death. They are *all* stories about the personal, individual journey of the soul from a state of unenlightened ignorance to cognizance of the divinity *within oneself.* The message of the Masters is one of unlimited love and caring *for all* regardless of origin. All are His, so the way to defuse tensions is to help all to see the unity and transcendence of God's message to all peoples. The consequence of religious illiteracy can be fatalities in clashes between religions, as we have seen all too many times in recent years, as well as down through history. Dangerous attitudes are created through ignorance, such as anticipation of a global "Armageddon" believed necessary to usher in a "Second Coming" of Christ, which is a complete misconstruing of an inner, personal, reality into an external, created one. Likewise is the belief that "Jihad" means "kill infidels" instead of the proper "conquer the lower mind." The only "Holy Land" is the real estate between and slightly above the eyes. The only "Holy War" is the one between the soul's higher and lower mind. Water baptism won't usher you into God's kingdom. Only the practice of the *"Word"* makes one holy. If we are to progress as a people, we all must strive to recognize our commonality, and acknowledge the common origin of disparate religious traditions. If one becomes aware of such widespread fundamental misunderstandings as are pointed out in this work, realizes the potential harm that they can cause, and can effect any sort of change for the better in comprehension of the truth, this writer believes it is a moral obligation to attempt to do so. There are many excellent works elsewhere covering this fascinating subject—some are listed below. To learn more, read the gnostic Nag Hammadi Library—its entirety is online at the Gnostic Society Library—and the other early Christian era apocrypha, Mandaean and Manichaean writings. The entire works of Josephus are also online.

Finally, illustrating the importance of Dr. Eisenman's contribution on the marginalization of James the Just in the Biblical canon, is this comment from an early draft of this book, written before reading his work: "The final step in bringing this revelation to a misled world is a complete scholarly survey of ancient manuscripts for documenting both the uninformed misrepresentation of mystic concepts as well as the telltale signs of additions, deletions, or changes to the texts showing the conscious intent to deceive and cover up the truth of Jesus Christ's limited ministry and true message (e.g., John 9:4 and 10:36, Psalm 22:16) and bringing these important facts to the attention of modern believers. We now call for and eagerly await the taking up of that momentous challenge. The advent of new information in the Dead Sea Scrolls and gnostic gospel collection demand it." What was not known to this writer was the extent to which it was the authors of the scriptures themselves who intended to deceive! Eisenman says one of the ways to prove a theory is to see if it has predictive value. That's what we find in examining Hebrew Matthew. A more ancient, uncorrupted source document closer in time to John and Jesus, and in one of their languages, should have a more authoritative view of John and Jesus' teachings—and it does. Thanks to Dr. Eisenman's work, we now know that the central importance of Jesus' brother, James, was intentionally and maliciously written out of the book of Acts and the Gospels, books taking their cue from the letters of Paul, who held an obvious animosity to James' teachings, teachings we know from recently unearthed pristine sources were heartily endorsed by the historical Jesus Christ. The continued misinformed idolizing of the Hellenized mystery-religion figure of the New Testament Jesus Christ does a disservice to the deep and abiding truths he, his cousin, and brothers brought to Roman Palestine at such high personal costs.

Appendix

Genesis 1:29: "And God said, 'Behold I have given you every plant yielding seed which is upon the face of all the earth, and every tree with seed in its fruit; you shall have them for food.'"

This discussion about Jesus Christ's true message cannot close without revisiting his vegetarianism. We have established that Jesus taught what is elsewhere called Surat Shabd Yoga, and have shown where to find the evidence for that in the Bible (John 4:24, 3:8, and Matthew 6:22). That means he was a vegetarian. The reasons for this, besides good health, are to avoid incurring heavy karmic debt, which hinders spiritual progress, and to avoid the infliction of suffering and unnecessary death on animals. God gave man *dominion* over "the fish of the sea, over the birds of the air, and over the cattle, and every creeping thing" (Gen. 1:26), He didn't tell him to EAT them. The statistics are staggering: According to USDA's National Agriculture Statistics Survey (NASS) reports and expert interviews, 9.7 billion animals were killed for food in the United States in 2000—mostly birds (9.5 billion chickens, turkeys and ducks), but also 42 million cows, 4 million sheep, and 115 million pigs. In more personal terms, the average American meat-eating man, woman, and child subsidize the farming and slaughter of thirty-seven animals per year. That's 2,800 animals in a seventy-five year lifetime. This number includes 2,630 chickens and ducks, 123 turkeys, 32 pigs, 13 cows and calves, and 2 sheep. None of these figures include seafood. When the devastation of fishing practices in the oceans is included, the scale of killing becomes difficult to comprehend: An estimated total of 94.8 million tons caught worldwide in 2000, including 4 million tons of tuna—now found primarily only in the Mediterranean Sea, 100 million sharks, 8 million tons of crabs, continued harvesting of whales by the Japanese, and millions of tons of wasted bycatch, including dolphins, porpoises, finned sharks, and sea turtles. Three-quarters of world fisheries are fished beyond sustainability, one-third are in active decline, salmon recently closed down, tuna nearly gone, Oyster beds 85 percent gone. Factory farming environmental damage to the land and air is devastating: Fuel and water consumption is enormous—75 percent of U.S. farmland topsoil *is gone*, 85 percent due to livestock grazing (source: Vegsource.com). Cattle produced methane greenhouse gas (95 percent orally!) is 21 times as potent as carbon dioxide, and at an estimated 100 million *tons* annually, is warming the planet (2.1 billion tons CO2 equivalent). The toll on ocean ecosystems by factory farming, herding (global warming, fertilizer and pesticide runoff, dust sedimentation on coral reefs), and fishing is catastrophic. The Chesapeake Bay is a deadzone from chicken farm operation runoff. The Mississippi drainage has killed an area the size of Massachusettes off the Louisiana coast. Abandoned fishing nets devastate non-target fish, marine mammals, and coral communities. Bottom trawling scours the seafloor of all life. Even vegetarians contribute: Government farming support is $114 billion annually, and $600 billion in government subsidies support food export processors; much for animal related farming. Yearly worldwide fishing industry government support is $15 billion, $100 million last year for Pacific coast salmon fishermen alone.

The point here is that we should not wonder at the bad things that we may have to endure in life, or be reborn to endure! Look no further than what is on your dinner plate for the source of your karma. (Even vegetable-eating creates karma—just less severely than meat-eating. This segment is not meant to be judgmental. I am not an animal rights PETA fanatic. I don't even approve of what they do. The dangers of meat-eating, however, are real. Since Pythagoras—the time of the Vedas, even—we have been warned of the consequences of causing harm to animals.) A recent federal study of a half million subjects in the U.S. found that substantial red meat consumption increases death risk 20-27 percent for cancer and 20-50 percent (up to 50 percent for women) for heart disease. Accompanying commentary also found livestock grazing to be a heavy contributor to global warming, and that government subsidies should end. Killing is a sin. "Thou shalt not *kill.*" (Exod. 20:13, Deut. 5:17). Slaughtering animals doesn't come naturally to most people, that's one reason others are hired to do it. The karmic debt incurred, however, must be settled—make no mistake about it. Man is not evolved to eat animal food (see "The Comparative Anatomy of Eating," by Dr. Milton Mills, Vegsource.com), nor is it countenanced by any true spiritual Master. According to Dr. Mills, the elevated and articulated jaw-joint (among other similar adaptations), which man possesses, is so vitally important to dedicated herbivores that it has evolved some fifteen times independently during evolutionary history for plant-eating. Compassion for all living creatures is a hallmark of the truly spiritual person. Without it, progress on the spiritual path is not possible. There is more than enough arable land to sustain a vegetarian world population, especially after one subtracts the land area and crops currently devoted to animal husbandry, which would probably leave a surplus of farming land, as well as a savings of water, power, and fertilizer used.

> "The greatness of a nation and its moral progress can
> be judged by the way its animals are treated."
> —Mahatma Gandhi

Selected Bibliography

1. Davidson, John, The Gospel of Jesus. Beas, India, Radha Soami Satsang Beas, 1995, 2004.
2. Del Tondo, Douglas, Jesus Words Only. West Conshohocken, PA, Infinity Publishing Co., 2006.
3. Ehrman, Bart D., Misquoting Jesus. New York, NY, Harper Collins Publishers, 2005.
4. Ehrman, Bart D., The Orthodox Corruption of Scripture. New York, NY, Oxford University Press, Inc., 1993.
5. Eisenman, Robert H., James, the Brother of Jesus. New York, NY, Penguin Group, Inc., 1997.
6. Eienman, Robert H., The Dead Sea Scrolls and the First Christians. Edison, NJ, Castle Books, 1996, 2006.
7. Eisenman, Robert H., The New Testament Code. London, England, Watkins Publishing, 2006.
8. Johnson, Dr. Julian, The Path of the Masters. Beas, India, Radha Soami Satsang Beas, 1939, 1980.
9. Pagels, Elaine, The Gnostic Gospels. Vintage Books, Edition 1989. New York, NY, Random House Inc., 1979.
10. Shanks, Hershel, Understanding the Dead Sea Scrolls. New York, NY, Random House, Inc., 1992

11. Singh, Maharaj Charan, Light on Saint John. Beas, India, Radha Soami Satsang Beas, 1967, 2007.

12. Singh, Maharaj Charan, Light on Saint Matthew. Beas, India, Radha Soami Satsang Beas, 1978.

13. Spong, John Shelby, Rescuing the Bible from Fundamentalism. San Francisco, CA, Harper San Francisco, 1992.

14. Spong, John Shelby, Resurrection: Myth or Reality? San Francisco, CA, Harper San Francisco, 1994.

15. Stone, Dr. Randolph, Mystic Bible. Beas, India, Radha Soami Satsang Beas, 1956, 1989 (Out of print).

16. Tabor, James, Jesus Dynasty. New York, New York, Simon & Schuster, 2006.

17. The Bible, Authorized Version (1611 King James Version). Cambridge, England, Cambridge University Press.

18. The Bible, Jerusalem Bible. London, England, Darton, Longman & Todd and Doubleday, 1966.

19. The Bible, Revised Standard Version. Camden, NJ, Thomas Nelson, Inc. National Council of the Churches of Christ in America, 1952.

20. The Gospel of Judas, Edited by Rodolphe Kasser, Marvin Meyer, and Gregor Wurst. Washington, D.C., National Geographic Society, 2006.

21. The Nag Hammadi Library, James M. Robinson, Editor. San Francisco, NY, Harper San Francisco, 1978, 1988.

22. Tulsi Sahib—Saint of Hathras. Beas, India, Radha Soami Satsang Beas, 1978.

23. Online Parallel Bible, http://bible.cc/

24. Five Gospels Parallels, http://www.utoronto.ca/religion/synopsis/

"Behold, I stand at *the door* [the 'single eye'] and knock; if any one hears *my voice* [the 'Word'] and opens the door, I will come in to him and eat with him, and he with me."

—Revelation 3:20

"And they shall *listen to the voice* [meditate on the 'Word'] of the Teacher of Righteousness and not desert the Laws of Righteousness. But rather, *when they hear them*, they shall exult and rejoice, and their hearts shall be Strengthened, and they shall prevail against all the Sons of the Earth [worldly spirits]. And God will make atonement for them, and they will see His Salvation [Yeshu'a], because they took refuge *in His Holy Name* [the 'Word']."

—Damascus Document, CD XX, Ms. B 32b-34

"and many peoples shall come and say:
'Come, let us go up to *the mountain
of the Lord* [the 'single eye'],
to the house of the God of Jacob;
that he may teach us his ways
and that we may walk in his paths.'
For out of Zion shall go forth the law,
and *the Word* of the Lord *from
Jerusalem* [Heaven]."
"Turn away from *man* [the body] in whose
nostrils is breath for of what account is he?"

—Isaiah 2:3, 22

Get Published, Inc!
Thorofare, NJ 08086
27 October 2009
BA2009240